CHARMERS
&
CON ARTISTS

& THEIR
FLIP SIDE...

CHARMERS
&
CON ARTISTS

& THEIR
FLIP SIDE...

SANDRA SCOTT

Pleasant W rd

Pleasant Word (a division of WinePress Publishing, PO Box 428, Enumclaw, WA 98022) functions only as book publisher. As such, the ultimate design, content, editorial accuracy, and views expressed or implied in this work are those of the author.

Unless otherwise noted all Scriptures are taken from the Holy Bible, King James Version, Copyright © 1611.

ISBN 13: 978-1-4141-0891-9
ISBN 10: 1-4141-0891-5
Library of Congress Catalog Card Number: 2006910114

written for those who hurt,
the charmed and the Charmer

DEDICATED TO

Sharon
Bonnie
Diane
Donna
Joyce
P. K.
Tonya
Gwen
Charlene
Carroll
Barbara

. . . and all the others.

CONTENTS

PREFACE

There are many people who unknowingly or knowingly allow themselves to be given over to evil – to using and abusing others. Many of them believe they are merely coping and surviving, so they feel no guilt. Some don't care. This is written to educate and teach appropriate, healing responses.

"All that is necessary for evil to prevail is that good men do nothing." . . . Edmund Burke

"Men who manipulate and violate others will never listen to their pain and pleas. They will only listen to good men who hold them accountable for their bad behavior. Where else should we expect to find a collection of good men but in the church and the courts?" . . . Sandra Scott

Ignorance is *never* bliss. What we don't know can and usually will hurt us. Truth often hurts as well, but in a cleansing, healing way.

Prophets, seers, and truth-tellers have never been popular. They make people uneasy. They make us feel exposed and vulnerable. When fun or pleasure are unveiled as destructive, the news is rarely welcomed. Wanting to "kill the messenger" is not uncommon, but it doesn't change the message.

The uglier the information seems to us or the more difficult the news is to believe, the greater becomes our human instinct to live in denial. The more important the information and the more persistent the deliverer, the more resistant the hearers are likely to become.

Those who watch and don't understand—the ones who don't see beyond the appealing surface—shake their heads and see the wronged one as delusional, paranoid, or meanspirited. They fall prey to sympathizing with the instigator in his crafty portrayal of his innocence. The result is invalidation of the victim's experience. Victims then doubt their own perception and even their sanity.

Meanwhile, both the perpetrators of evil and the onlookers grow in their disdain for the revealer of the reality. It spoils their comfortable lethargy and the lull in which they suspend and numb their awareness. This is particularly true when some of the most charismatic and likable people are unmasked as dangerous to be around. Charmers and con artists are so appealing, so soothing to the spirit, and they are such desirable agents of a feel-good society, we really don't want to know we are being fooled. How could it be so wrong, when it "feels" so right?

Regardless of the cost, we *must* be made aware. The price of not seeing or hearing truth is too great. Not knowing can put us in harm's way. It can rob us of our dignity, our integrity, and endanger our very souls.

PREFACE

As an educator and a professional, I am on a quest to provide information to those reluctant to know—information without which anyone is a potential victim of seduction. I have encountered great resistance to this information from the people who are in the best positions to help and advocate for victims: the courts, law enforcement, clergy, and employers.

Sometimes there are loved ones—people to whom a victim needs to turn—who can't grasp what they are hearing and have no idea of how to help. Most alarming has been that there are many in the mental health field whose knowledge is sorely limited. Ignorance allows Charmers, con artists, and abusers to exist and flourish.

The purpose of this book is to identify Charmers and warn readers of the Charmer's threat to them. It is also intended to validate and help those drawn in and hurt by Charmers. Finally, the information here is offered to allow Charmers to see themselves at a crossroads at which they can make a choice: either to move toward integrity, or to continue in deepening pathology. Unfortunately, most Charmers cannot or are not willing to choose the first alternative, since they believe they are getting their needs met.

I speak from personal experience with both a Charmer and a con artist. It was only after my own recovery and after observing similar patterns in others' stories, that I realized what my own journey had truly been. This realization marked the beginning of understanding the road I had traveled.

A reader can greatly misunderstand or misuse this book. It is important for anyone who starts it, to finish it; otherwise, those who identify with the information could become discouraged. My purpose is to provide awareness and healing for both the charmed and the Charmer.

Don't be discouraged if you just don't "get it" or if you do see it but just can't break free of your situation. As you read, you may discover that you've "been there" or that you "are there." Facing such a reality and dealing with it is not an easy process but you are not alone. Perhaps this book will plant the seed from which your courage will grow.

This information offended a number of people when I introduced it. Interestingly, most of those who were offended were not Charmers. They were simply afraid I was criticizing some of their dating-and-mating techniques, and they feared becoming ineffective or looking foolish in their relationships. This is not about the healthy, age-old, male-female mating dance. It is about misuse of that process, whether in romantic or other relationships. Another group of people who were apprehensive about discussion of this subject were those who knew full well that they *do* take advantage of people, and they feared exposure. Then there were some Charmer-types who listened to and even agreed with the information, either believing that they would not be recognized by others or thinking that it did not apply to them, since they did not see themselves clearly.

The case studies I use are an amalgamation of many stories from many sources. Parts are fictional examples, except in the cases of well-known people, which have already been well documented. Otherwise, the names, places, and other identifiable parts have been changed. Any similarity with actual people or situations is purely coincidental.

Individuals who have been duped already, recognize and applaud this work, while lamenting that they didn't know earlier the information it contains. To those people who have trusted me by sharing the experiences and heartaches they have had with a Charmer or con artist, I am grateful. It is for them and other potential victims that I have written this work, and it is to them it is dedicated.

INTRODUCTION

Wisdom begins with knowledge.
Knowledge empowers.

There is a story of a frog placed in a beaker of cold water over a low flame in a laboratory. The water warmed slowly, one degree at a time. Since frogs are cold-blooded animals, this frog started out very comfortably, but gradually it began to die without even realizing what was happening. There was no struggle, just a gentle drifting into death. There was probably even a degree of contentment . . . until it was too late.

This illustrates what happens to many people who are lulled into a seemingly blissful (usually exciting) relationship with a Charmer. All the while, they think they are happy and having the time of their lives, only to find, over time, that they have lost themselves. Usually there is a lack of tangible evidence to the contrary, and with the subtleties of the circumstances, they begin to doubt themselves, their perceptions, and their own ability to discern reality or to improve their situation.

The Charmer doesn't win in the long run either. The same frog illustration applies to him or her. The seeming success he experiences makes him believe life is working for him. But his life is marked by emptiness and a lack of real intimacy with others. His is an emotional and spiritual death.

What makes this so tragic is that the Charmer either does not know or does not let anyone else know the inner workings of his life so that he can get help. Charmers are resistant to the very information that could set them free. The danger for them is that theirs is behavior that usually escalates, since the rewards increase and further forestall consequences.

The ones the Charmer is hurting don't realize what they are dealing with and are so emotionally addicted to the Charmer that they either can't get themselves free, or they are so lost in the ecstasy of the high, that they don't even want to know they are at risk. Frequently, a wiser friend or family member sees the reality and tries to warn the believer, only to be rebuffed.

A Charmer is not a diagnosis found in the *DSM IV*[1] (the diagnostic manual used by all mental health professionals). It is my own "tag" for a personality type best identified by this descriptive term. It *does not* refer to nice people who are charming.

I first became acquainted with the word *Charmer* (in psychological terms) through discussing a case with a colleague. A charismatic, personable husband, described by most people as "just the nicest guy you could ever know," was also very subtle in his control of the relationship and had an unsettling ability to be both self-serving and irresponsible toward his commitments. His wife, quite oblivious to the paradox, seemed puzzled by how much anger she was feeling. She was impatient with herself and felt guilty because of the anger she was directing at her wonderful husband. The marriage was no longer working for them, and the woman accepted the blame herself, even though the evidence didn't support her conclusions.

When my friend, with whom I was discussing this case, tagged the husband as "a Charmer," I asked for a prognosis for him and the marriage. Her response was discouraging and caught me quite off guard. "It's negative," she said. "Charmers don't come in for therapy. If they do, it's only to placate someone. They don't see a problem, because life works for *them*, so why should they change? If they do come in, they don't stay in therapy—unless they succeed in also charming the therapist."

With a sense of helplessness as a counselor, feelings of sympathy for the wife, and dread for the marriage, I set out to learn all I could about Charmers. I began collecting case studies, looking for common threads to provide clues.

First I realized that *nice* does not always mean what the speaker intends. *Likable* or *lovable* may be more appropriate. *Nice* denotes a person whose walk equals his talk; it speaks of good values and behaviors.

I found that divorce devastated the partners of Charmers, and they were unable to recover normally. Many of them, years later, were still trying to figure out what had happened. They suffered far more self-doubt, low self-esteem, loss, and guilt than did others who went through divorce.

For those who did not divorce or separate from their Charmer, they lived with a level of sad acceptance and self-blame. The only way they could continue was with a level of denial, suppressing feelings of confusion, anger, and self-abandonment. They had greater bouts with depression. They had moments of highs, sharing life with an exciting, life-on-the-edge spouse, but the payoff was a great many more very low times. They found themselves entangled in a web, seduced into the spiral of addiction from which they knew they should extricate themselves. They feared facing a mind-boggling recovery process if they did. Fear of the unknown was greater than their suppressed pain. Only the fleeting highs they could grasp here and there offset the pain of staying.

I began noticing how many public figures and those who make the headlines fit into the profile. I saw similar characteristics in people who were abusive—whether it was physical abuse in domestic violence, murderous rage, destruction of public or private property or the breaking of other laws, or whether it was in the more subtle techniques of stalking, harassment, verbal or emotional abuse. The latter style seemed more the arena of the Charmer. I found many Charmers were abusers in private. They were masters of charm in persuading their victims to trust them again.

Addictions and abuse are both ultimately about *control*. Addiction is a desperate attempt to seize control by someone who feels out-of-control in his life. His substance (or activity) provides temporary feelings of relief and euphoria. When the rush is gone or unfulfilling, the cycle begins again with a greater need than before. It is the only disease that successfully convinces the diseased that he is not afflicted.

The blatant abuser lacks the Charmer's skills and ability to gain control willingly from the victim, so he bullies, intimidates, and uses force. When the Charmer's charm no longer works, he will usually just move on, knowing there are vast opportunities for him elsewhere. However, if there is a lot at stake for him—a relationship or job he needs or the protection of his public image—he will feel justified in forcing his agenda. He will redouble his efforts to use his skills, but to the extent that the goal is important to him and that his skills are no longer effective, he will become abusive.

A favorite technique of the Charmer is to be passive-aggressive. The pay off for this approach is his ability to control his environment by doing nothing and quietly orchestrating the frantic choreography of those around him, thereby avoiding responsibility for the results, but being the primary beneficiary.

The research led to new questions:

- What's the difference between being charming and being a Charmer?
- How does one become a Charmer?
- Is a Charmer truly happy?
- Does a Charmer know he's a Charmer?
- What about his conscience? His integrity?
- What's the difference between a Charmer and a con artist?

For those who have had a Charmer in their lives, there was immediate identification with my research. They may not have had a name for it before, but there was relief in having someone finally put a label on their experience.

For Charmers, this information will create different reactions, including pain and disappointment, depending on their level of integrity. There are degrees of being a Charmer that run along a continuum, from the obvious silver-tongued Lothario or backslapping salesman, to the more diabolical and pathological examples of Ted Bundy or Adolph Hitler, with accompanying levels of destruction and victimization.

Not everyone who gets charmed gets hurt. Usually it's the people closest to a Charmer who suffer: his inner circle, those who are up close and personal, his captive audience. That usually means family members or those whom the Charmer needs most. The ones who enjoy an association with the Charmer and pay little or no price are usually part of the Charmer's general public, one of his many audiences. Those people find it hard to believe anyone would not feel the same sense of fun, excitement, and privilege that they do. Since they haven't been close enough to the flame to get singed, burned, or consumed, these people on the periphery envy those in the Charmer's inner circle.

But for those—both Charmers and their victims—caught in the unending dance, there is a sense of elation as well as of confusion. Everything looks so good on the outside, but inside is an unfilled cavern. People who have a contrary, secret inner life and obsessions are not healthy, happy people, no matter what their facade.

To be charming is a wonderful, admirable attribute. That's not the same as operating as a Charmer. Being in the company of the Charmer is very appealing. They are usually attractive people (or appealing in some way) with great communication skills, though not necessarily verbal. They may be easily identified or be very subtle in their demeanor. But there is a difference in what we think we see and what's really there. There's a difference between being charming and being a Charmer. There's a difference between having charisma and being a user.

To say a person is charming conjures images of someone who is warm, easygoing, amiable, gracious—someone who knows the appropriate response to anyone in any situation. Such a person is smooth, has an air of confidence, yet demonstrates a caring sensitivity to others. The French say he is *debonair*, that he has *savoir-faire*. He's the spoonful of sugar that helps the medicine of life go down.

The Charmer, however, can be harmful to the mental and emotional health of those closest to him, and eventually to his own well-being. He is charming, but instead of his charm being an outward expression of his inner self, there is, under the surface, an ulterior purpose for his own gain.

Unless you've had first-hand experience, you probably wouldn't recognize a Charmer or understand the hurt he or she can cause. Nor will you likely identify with any of this unless you or someone close to you has already been hurt. And if you are a Charmer, you may not realize the truth about yourself unless you know the characteristics and identify with the things that motivate and typify a Charmer.

Some charmers, such as a Ted Bundy at one extreme, are eventually exposed and suffer the consequences. Then there are those, such as O. J. Simpson, who we discover have lived two different lives: a charming public image that effectively concealed a darker side at home with immediate family members. Many Charmers may not abuse to the point of actually breaking the law (e.g., John Kennedy's breaking his word and betraying his wife with his infidelities), but there are those who will bend or break laws and rules of society to effectively cover or get away with their behavior (e.g., Bill Clinton). It's this kind of excitement that makes them feel vibrant, alive, and in control of their realm. (I must make it clear, at this point, that this is not a party issue; regardless of your political alignment, Kennedy and Clinton are the two politicians about whom the most has been written recently, thus identifying them with this subject.)

All Charmers are very good at walking the edge of the line that would expose them. It's their "high." They are risk takers and can talk out of both sides of their mouths as needed. They are also able to compartmentalize what they do, so they see no relevance of behavior in one area to that of other parts of their lives. They truly see themselves as victims— "the good guys."

It is rare, and with great effort on the part of someone else, that a Charmer is finally exposed. Yet, even after he is exposed, a Charmer will not recognize the truth about himself, and interestingly, the one who exposes a Charmer is usually attacked as the problem and suffers the loss of his own credibility, well-being, and even safety. Such a person risks a great deal trying to help.

Regardless of the proofs presented, there are still legions of people who will refuse to believe evidence that reveals the truth about a Charmer's deceptions. These people prefer the comfort of their delusion. The Charmer is their champion. He or she represents the pinnacle of the human experience—that of being in control of one's own realm, of being on top of the heap.

At the other end are the Charmers who manage to spread themselves so thin that hardly anyone gets close to them. They are the ones, with the tentative smile, that are surprised to discover they are actually bleeding and can't quite figure out how it all happened. Their relationships are all so shallow and hit-and-run, that they never allow any feedback on their behavior. They leave hurting people, broken relationships, and devastation in their wake—for someone else to clean up, if it's repairable at all.

To get his *needs* met—to survive, at least in his own mind—the Charmer operates as a "people pleaser." He must manipulate others to get what he needs. As we will see later, the con artist is a "people pleaser," as well, but operates this way to get what he *wants*. He has a broader goal in mind.

NOTE: The term *Charmer* includes the con artist only when describing methods of operation both Charmer and con artist may employ. However, the two are indicated separately when describing the person or his/her motives or goals.

(Because Charmers are more often male than female, most references and pronouns in this work are rendered in the masculine. This is not an indictment, but rather a convenience in writing and reading. Please recognize that references here also apply to female Charmers. Male or female, except for a few variations due to gender, the descriptions remain the same for both.)

CHARMING? A CHARMER?
OR A CON ARTIST?

DESCRIPTION AND PROFILE
OF A CHARMER

H E'S THE PIED PIPER you cannot resist following, even when he steps out of the way to safety and leads his followers over a cliff and into a vast abyss. He's Peter Pan with promises to take you to Never-Never Land where you'll never have to grow up. He's exciting and irresistible.

He believes he is special and that it takes a special person to understand his specialness. He makes you believe you are special too, because you are able to understand him. This hooks you into supporting and defending him without question, ignoring evidence or comments to the contrary. He has an excuse or reason for everything. He has his own brand of logic that is seductively convincing in getting you to believe in him and his rationale.

He is subtle in soliciting special privileges with his winning smile, his piercing eye-contact, or his obvious interest in you, any of which seem to overshadow his meager request for accommodation. You see, the same rules that apply to others should not restrict him. He wants you to bend them or suspend them. All the while, he has you believing you are being generous, magnanimous, or more understanding than others.

He has an unusual talent for ingratiating himself to others, and he easily picks up on the special interests of others or their vulnerabilities and plays to them. He knows how to appear to be the giver; in fact, he may do a lot of giving. What you can't see is that the price you will pay later will be greater than the value you receive from him.

But who thinks about tomorrow's hangover while enjoying tonight's party? He is intoxicating to be around. Things happen; excitement reigns. You believe *you* are on the receiving end and that he is your benefactor. You feel on top of world.

Sooner or later, though, you begin to realize that these feelings are being offset by bouts of depression, anger, inadequacy. You experience a lowering of your self-esteem and a diminishing confidence in your perception of people and circumstances. You believe that it must be you. It couldn't be him!

Your feelings are getting hurt—deeply and frequently—but it will be a long time before you see that, because he *can't* feel love deeply, neither can he feel deep guilt or pain, especially that of others. In fact, if you question the Charmer's behavior or express your ill-treatment, these concerns are minimized or dismissed. Whenever the Charmer is caught or confronted on any behavior, he or she expects always to be forgiven, without consequences or really resolving anything. The Charmer can apologize at the drop of a hat, with a straight face, and not mean a word of it.

The better and more accomplished the Charmer, the longer it will take for anyone to uncover the truth. He will usually move on to other devotees and try to discredit his accusers. This may even come in the form of an apology but with the underlying message, "Well, that's their perception, but I'll be the bigger person and take the responsibility, rather than expose them or be unkind to them." He's very good at making himself the hero in even the worst situation.

Or a Charmer can really mean he is sorry, but that's as far as it goes. That's the end of it as far as he is concerned. No one has the right to monitor his behavior to see if it is consistent with his promises. He may truly, sincerely apologize but have no intention of accepting any real consequences or making real amends. He may do something significant to make it look real, or even make it real, if it gets him something bigger as a payoff. Even his remorse is manipulative and short-lived, and there is never true repentance.

He never intends really to change anything that works for him. He may disguise it next time, learning from his mistakes, so he won't be caught again. He may even tell you there will be no "next time." But there will be. It's the way he lives. Why should he change? Even when he really means to change (to make his life work even better for him), he's all but incapable. Years of repetition, of believing his own hero image, and of a surface level of self-satisfaction have become so ingrained that he operates automatically.

Eventually, you begin to see that he is the one benefiting from *your* support and devotion and what they buy for him. You may start catching him in lies and deception in many forms, and you may notice his increasingly obvious and blatant demands on everything and everyone around him. You notice that your choices, your needs, your desires all give way to pleasing or being with him. And you have done it willingly. You wake up to find you've lost yourself somewhere along the yellow brick road.

He appears to like everyone and to be very likable. He seems to have all the right moves and words in social situations. Many Charmers will have a sterling reputation, while others are the disarming, playful, naughty rogue. He may be smooth, or he may present himself in the least suspicious way: as a self-effacing, even bumbling, needy individual. All are designed to draw you in. He may be admired or aggressively sought after by others. If you get close enough, however, the charm will eventually take on a macabre appearance. It will begin to sting and then devour you.

Being a Charmer has little to do with intelligence, but more to do with cleverness. Charmers are at both ends of that spectrum. Their quest for survival is at a base, impulsive level; it has become instinctive. It is at the same level as the animal kingdom. A higher level of intelligence or accomplishment merely provides access to a higher level audience.

Charmers count on others to be too gracious, too well-mannered, too mature, or too kind to confront them, so they continue to be able to get away with their behavior. They are also adept at turning around any challenge to make the accuser appear petty, jealous, delusional, judgmental, or rude. If someone doesn't support them, they are able to make it look like "sour grapes" on the other person's part. The absence of confrontation is interpreted by them as approval of what they do.

They will usually have a series of broken or shallow relationships. The more shallow a life is lived, the more easily it becomes bored and needs to seek more extreme (and often perverse) ways to stimulate, titillate, and be satisfied.

They like to see how close to the edge they can get and still survive or even win. Like the children of alcoholics or other dysfunction, they gravitate to a well-known, comfortable scenario that will produce in them a familiar feeling, even if it is very short in duration and even if they hate it and it makes them miserable. It's what they are used to and the only thing they believe they can effectively handle.

Without realizing it, they are on a self-destructive path. They know they are isolated and lonely; they can't face that, so they cover up any way they can. This makes them prime candidates for addictions: substance abuse, gambling, excessive activity or recreation, workaholism, sexual addiction, and anything else they can use to fill the vacuum or provide a quick fix.

Most Charmers will demonstrate extreme shifts in personality: high/low, kindness/sarcasm, etc. Their negative side is usually covert, or it may show itself in humor that is cynical or at someone else's expense.

A Charmer depends on the reputation of his converts to carry him if he gets caught. His remaining defenders will turn on any accuser, usually with great venom. A Charmer is amazingly proficient at getting those who continue to believe in him to defend him "to the death"—whether it means loss of career or reputation—even after evidence of their delusion has been revealed. What is pathetic about those believers is that they actually think the Charmer cares about them. They don't see they are being used. Believers don't recognize their own need to believe that someone has "made it"—has taken charge of life—as the Charmer appears to have done. That fantasy gives them hope for themselves.

When things begin to unravel, believers may start to wonder if they're going crazy. They may think they're becoming delusional or paranoid. They can't bear to believe their trust has been misplaced and that they've been played for a fool. So pride or pain persuades them to go on believing the unbelievable.

"Am I the only one who senses that something is wrong here?" you ask yourself. "Am I jealous, overly sensitive, or too critical? It must be me since I appear to be the only one who sees it." But, it's more than puzzling. It's feeling drained, having life siphoned from you. Yet this seems so inconsistent with what everyone around you thinks. They believe you are fortunate to be in the inner circle of one so revered.

The Charmer accelerates his skills on those who challenge him. With those people, the Charmer will periodically test the limits to which he can go and yet win out. These victims are given subtle messages that nothing they do is quite good enough. They are being taught that they, not the Charmer, are the problem. Actually, the Charmer is a bottomless pit of need, but the message he conveys is that it is someone else's fault for not being able to fill him up. His defense is to go on the offense:

- "You are imagining things."
- "You are being overly sensitive."
- "You just don't understand."
- "Can't you just go along with things?"
- "Can't you take a joke?"
- "I'm doing the best I can!" (This one leaves you stuck feeling and looking ungrateful.)
- "What about what *you* are doing?"

Or he will sweetly apologize for his behavior, but you both know it will not be the last time. Past experience has taught you that he believes if he says the magic words, "I'm sorry," everything will be fine. He then sees he has a clean slate, without any consequence or reference to the infraction and without any amends being made.

The pattern will leave you, once again, optimistic that it will be different next time, hoping there will never be a next time, believing because you want desperately to believe. You defend his behaviors, rationalizing violations of moral and legal rules. But in the end, you feel inadequate and inaccurate in assessing what you see, hear, and feel. It leaves you doubting yourself and your concept of reality.

Instead of getting angry at the Charmer's manipulation of you and your perception of a situation, you feel ashamed at not seeing things more clearly, and you feel guilty for challenging him and making a big deal out of it. You are led to believe you are a troublemaker, an alarmist, or a poor sport. The message is that *you* are the problem.

To stay in good graces or to avoid the wrath of their Charmer, victims end up compromising their own value system and what they know to be right. They live with a cancerous guilt that erodes their life, their individuality, and their very spirit.

The Charmer *appears* to have great sensitivity to others and to *understand* all *about* feelings—both his own and those of others. He seems to have invisible antennae to grasp onto the people who will respond positively to him. These same antennae tell him exactly what will appeal to and win that person to himself and just how far he can go with it.

He is a genius at imitating virtue and portraying himself publicly in a very positive light. It makes him very appealing company. He usually possesses a ready sense of humor and can tell a good story or do something to make others laugh or feel good. His particular method of operation may be to be a wonderful, adoring listener, letting the other person shine for the moment, endearing himself to them.

A Charmer is a master at ingratiating himself to others. He has a "Ted Kennedy style of leadership": he assesses which way the wind is blowing, steps out in front of everyone, and yells, "Follow me!"

But real feelings (apart from those surrounding his own fears) are a limited or absent experience for a Charmer. He operates at a surface level with well-developed communication skills in lieu of expressing at a real or deep level. The feelings he does allow are the ones that directly affect himself. In place of real empathy for someone's pain, he may feel frustrated or sad at the inconvenience it causes him. He may even be skillful at feigning empathy and saying, "I feel your pain." While he might say the right words, his motive (though others may never know it) is always his own welfare.

As a result, genuine intimacy is a remote possibility for the Charmer; although he allows and encourages others to feel intimacy toward him. He's a good pretender, and he may even feel emotionally intimate for brief periods of time or fleeting moments.

Charmers are limited in their ability to truly love anyone. Love is to want, encourage, and support another person to be all he or she can be, which is to realize their full human potential. It is to value them, to be honest with them, to remain committed for the long haul, and to be concerned for and contribute to their needs and welfare beyond your own desires.

The Charmer fears having a victim realize his or her full human potential. While the victim is growing, he or she may uncover the truth about the Charmer's shallowness and his lack of ability to have a reciprocal relationship. The Charmer's existence depends on the victim's denial of the dysfunctional nature of the relationship, or their relationship will cease to exist. Therefore, the affection of a Charmer is not truly love but a tool for manipulation.

Because of the charmer's shallow relationships, he fears feelings below a surface level. That would make him vulnerable. That means taking emotional risks. (Many who are grandiose about taking physical or financial risks are compensating for their inability to take emotional risks.) Numbing, denying, or suppressing feelings gives the Charmer a belief that he is not accountable or responsible. He believes that if he doesn't acknowledge the feeling, the information, or the problem, there is no obligation to deal with or change anything. The Charmer will then dump them onto someone else. This passive aggressive behavior begins a round of rationalizing, projecting, or blaming. It is then easy for him to think or say, "That's their problem, not mine."

Just saying that, does not mean it's true. What it really means is this: "It is their problem to deal with; I choose not to." Thus, the mess is left for someone else, while the Charmer walks away with no feeling of guilt or remorse, oblivious to the inconvenience, hurt, frustration, anger, humiliation, or debt that they have left. The victim then looks hysterical or out of control with his or her feelings and with the task of smoothing out the situation. Charmers believe they've left nothing behind; it just magically disappeared. They manage to stay just out of reach, to move just at the moment of reckoning.

The Charmer looks for shortcuts, and to him, the end justifies the means. Not owning a problem, however, does not relinquish ownership; it merely transfers temporarily one's belief about the problem. The problem remains to be faced later when it resurfaces, as it must. By then, it may have a different face, have a different form, or have been pushed onto someone else. The Charmer survives only because of his ability to shift attention, either onto himself (if that's his need at the moment) or onto someone or something else, to divert scrutiny of his motives or behavior when such scrutiny might injure his image.

For instance, in a family where anger is not allowed to be appropriately expressed, a boy may have ongoing, unresolved anger. If he projects that anger onto his mother and it is never resolved, sooner or later he will project it onto a girlfriend, a wife, or all women. He may tend to overreact to even a small infraction. If his anger is at his father, he may choose to emulate that parent in order to "best" him. In some cases, such a man will need an inordinate amount of male bonding throughout life to fill the need for a good relationship with another man.

Unresolved anger in people will be spilt onto whomever is perceived as being weaker or more vulnerable than themselves at the moment. People who struggle in this way need to feel in control, so they do it by being controlling of others. One of the techniques a man may use for gaining control may be to become a "ladies' man." What better way to control and extract vengeance?

If a girl is the victim of emotional or physical incest by a parent, she may see herself as worthless, since the one who is supposed to love and protect her has abused her by drawing her into an inappropriate role. Chances are good that she will never be allowed to express her rage (or any other feelings, for that matter). Without that emotional outlet, and without having her feelings validated by someone, she may then decide she's not worthy of good treatment. Many such women become prostitutes, promiscuous, or homosexual, all of which can provide a false sense of being the one in control of a relationship. They can also become easy prey for Charmers.

When a child's needs are not met by his or her caregivers, that child's survival instincts take over, doing whatever it takes to get those needs met. Many are able to rise above such obstacles to become the person, the parent, the friend, they didn't have. The less productive survival methods of childhood usually become the problems of adulthood. One method is to escape into addictions to ease the pain. The Charmer is addicted to self-preservation. His unmet needs must find expression, compassion, grieving, and healing in order for him to let them go in exchange for healthy responses. The healthy person is able to see those issues as childish solutions which need to be reevaluated and replaced with adult wisdom. Charmers remain locked in the childish fears, which they go on covering with more sophisticated, acceptable ways of surviving.

Charmers are people who have learned to use their personal appeal and interpersonal skills to rescue themselves from what they believe to be stressful or dangerous situations. The better those skills work for them and the longer they have used them, the more perfected they have become at being Charmers, not really learning to problem-solve or deal honestly with life.

Charmers are not content people. They appear very successful in their lives, but *they* know they are limited in certain ways. They put all their faith and confidence in their ability to manipulate people and events. Their inner fear is that they will meet those along the way who will see through their facade and refuse to be manipulated. They run away from those people. They do anything they can to dismiss them from their lives or to discredit them.

Charmers rarely allow themselves in-depth self-examination or opportunity for feedback to realize what they are doing. Moments of stress or confrontation may uncover it, but Charmers are very good at avoiding both of these things or at quickly losing any memory of them.

They have learned how to maintain a false self—a public image and a "hero" self-image, which reflect a pseudo happiness that even they have come to believe. Because they are not in touch with many feelings nor experiencing feelings at any real depth, they have low self-esteem. They don't really know their true "self." They don't enjoy being alone unless in hiding or pouting. They crave attention or adoration or just being around people to reassure themselves that they are functioning and in control of life.

Interestingly, when this information is presented in a noncondemning way, some Charmers may open up to take a serious look at their lives and will have great sadness about the methods they've used and how it makes them feel about themselves. For them, it can become a moment of truth, a change of direction, and a reclaiming or establishing of a healthy, fully functioning person. The individual level of maturity and integrity will determine a Charmer's openness.

Just looking at the behaviors discussed thus far, it becomes evident that the main issue for the Charmer is one of immaturity, which focuses on self. It is the picture of one stuck in adolescence or earlier childhood. In the process of growing up, one learns an increasing vocabulary of feelings. One of the most important emotions and signs of maturing is an ever-growing sense of empathy—the ability to see things from another person's perspective and to equate their feelings with your own. For the Charmer, even viewing someone else's pain will really only invoke the awfulness for himself if he were in that same situation, rather than the pain *the other person* is feeling. A growing, maturing individual also becomes comfortable in feeling and managing the emotions they're developing, learning the difference between appropriate and inappropriate responses to one's own feelings, as well as a sensitivity to the feelings of others.

The case studies that follow will illustrate varying degrees of being a Charmer, as people in general have varying levels of maturity and integrity. Some Charmers are more dangerous than others. Some are more subtle than others. Those factors both determine and depend on how effectively they operate. Some are better at their skills than others. Some are physically more attractive than others, which enhances their appeal and ability to be effective. Some stay in one place too long until someone catches on and perhaps exposes them. This may push them to move on to another audience, to change or accelerate their tactics and strategy, or to become abusive if moving on isn't feasible. The greater degree to which one is a Charmer, the closer to pathology—*pathology* meaning "a character disorder or mental illness."

The fortunate ones face themselves and turn toward healthy recovery. However, their numbers are few because there are so many comfortable exits.

DIFFERENCES BETWEEN
CHARMER AND CON ARTIST

THE WORD *CHARM* originally referred to "an incantation" or "something assumed to have magical power to help or hurt," or as a verb, it meant "to enchant, allure, fascinate." It had to do with words and behaviors, not feelings. Right away, the definition gives a sense of unreality or falseness. To be charming is a desirable quality. It is a single attribute among many that can describe an individual. Of course, Charmers are indeed charming, but there are far more people who are very charming who are not Charmers.

We use many of these words loosely and interchangeably, without differentiating their real meanings. We might see a precocious child using his or her charm to bend the will of an adult. But both are fully aware of the game being played, and it's all right for the moment. We may say, "What a little charmer!" We might even say, "What a little con artist!" But we know what is going on. The child may naively believe he's really fooling someone, but the reality is playful for the adults.

A real Charmer or con artist, in the sense in which this book discusses them, is serious and has not informed the other party of the rules of his game. He's made a bargain, which no one else has consciously acknowledged and to which no one but himself has agreed. A Charmer is motivated more by a sense of entitlement and the need for a good image than by the need for gain (although material gain can certainly be part of it). The Charmer's view of any gain is that it is necessary for his security or that it is payment for injustices done to him.

The Charmer is one who has raised being charming to an art form, using charm as his disguise with which to manipulate people or situations for his own benefit. It's the degree to which one uses this behavior to define himself, or to be defined by others, that says one is a Charmer. The charm becomes a means to an end, rather than only one of many attributes describing a person. It goes from being an adjective to being a noun. The Charmer has *become* the characteristic in the same way one can move from feeling anger to becoming or functioning as an angry person. It defines who they are, how they respond to the world, the underlying definition of their personhood.

As mentioned earlier, the greater the level of being a Charmer, the less likely one is to recognize himself as such. As in any dysfunction, the more distracted an individual becomes in the use of the addictive substance or behavior, the better that person gets at hiding or disguising dependency, the less objective he becomes, and the more difficult it is to convince him of what is happening. Lies and deception become a total way of life.

A Charmer and a con artist are similar and different. Their method of operation is the same, but their motives and goals are different. The Charmer's driving force is need, survival. His goal is security, acceptance. His need for power is only to secure his goals. The con artist is motivated by his wants. His goal is usually material gain or power: sheer greed and sloth. There is often a blurred line between the Charmer and the con artist. Some people go back and forth between the two, able to function as one or the other, depending on the situation. The con artist knows full well he has the skills to manipulate, and he chooses to use those skills to his full personal advantage.

When the con is not conning someone, he can exhibit selective conscience and choose to bestow real kindness when he pleases. An example is a gangster who has and shows genuine love, affection, and protection for his own family members or friends, but who can also readily kill a stranger or enemy. He knows what he's doing, what his goal is, and that what he is doing is wrong. However, he doesn't care. He has made a decision to do it anyway. It isn't that he has no ethics. He has chosen to reject accepted ethical standards in favor of his own code of ethics.

The con artist has a fully developed conscience. He knows right from wrong but chooses wrong. He easily disguises his wrongs, and by the time he's discovered, he's usually long gone. The Charmer's conscience is underdeveloped and is only selective in that it decides what situation will benefit his own needs or image. He really believes he's not hurting anyone, since he's not feeling pain. His eyes are closed, so he believes no one can see him either. He is able to deny and avoid having to look at the impact of his actions on others.

If a Charmer is confronted with absolute proof of his behavior (to the point of positive recognition) and he is unwilling to change, then he has crossed the line and become, or really was all along, a con artist. He has made a conscious choice. He is no longer eligible for the excuses of ignorance or survival expediency. He is ineligible for any compassion or any more chances.

The con artist can rob you of your time, energy, and money. The Charmer can rob you of your youth, your integrity, your self-esteem, your very soul. The Charmer is more lethal but is also more pitiable than the con artist. He has a pain the con artist never knows. The con artist robs and leaves you sadder but wiser. The Charmer rapes your spirit and drags you with him into his own personal hell.

Shame, too, is an important difference between the Charmer and the con artist.

A sense of healthy shame about our imperfections is part of having a conscience and social sensitivity. It is appropriate to feel embarrassment if someone walks in while you are changing clothes, using the toilet, or making love. There's nothing wrong with any of it; it is a matter of modesty and privacy.

Human beings, in our imperfection, all have some level or type of neurosis. It is part of our personalities and makes us interesting to each other. [It's a reality that reminds me of a time I took a diamond to a jeweler for appraisal. He looked very serious as he said to me, "Well, it's flawed." Then he smiled and added, "But so are all my friends, and they are still very valuable."]

The neurotic goes overboard at times, experiencing undue shame about doing things which he believes he should not do or, on the other hand, about not doing what he believes he should do. This is what John Bradshaw calls *toxic shame*: inappropriate shame or guilt that someone else has laid on you and that you accept as true, such as the belief that your body, its functions, or appropriate sexual activity are things of which you should be ashamed.

The Charmer has a distorted view of shame. He has a toxic inappropriate sense of shame regarding his needs. He does not know how to get them met appropriately or in a healthy way. The Charmer's view of life is that it is happening *to him*; therefore, he must react defensively to survive and make life work well for himself. Whatever he believes will work for him, will become his tools.

He feels justified in what he does, so he has no embarrassment or sense of healthy shame about doing whatever is necessary to get his needs satisfied. The degree to which one indulges this thinking, determines where he or she is on the continuum toward crossing over the line of sanity. The farther along the continuum, the less ability a Charmer has to love anything or anyone.

The con artist knows the difference, but in choosing to do wrong, he automatically refuses the appropriate shame (or guilt) attached to inappropriate actions. Again, one is a choice based on ignorance, the other is a choice based on not caring. The Charmer projects feelings he believes he has, in order to make himself feel good. The con artist projects feelings he knows he doesn't have in order to win the confidence of others.

There have always been Charmers and con artists. But there are periods of time in a society in which moral voices are more silent than others, depending on what is politically correct at the time. This provides the perfect breeding ground for narcissism, which is the basis of the Charmer's existence. Our nation has gone through such a time in the past few decades.

Our society bought into the narcissistic notion during the "me" generation. In the years from the late sixties through the early eighties, how often did we hear "As long as I'm not hurting anyone else, I can do what I want"? It became easy to rationalize and justify one's behavior by issuing a blanket statement that people were islands unto themselves and that the rest of humanity was not in any way influenced by their choices. This generation's declaration of abdication was sufficient in its own mind, but only in its mind.

Unfortunately, so many said it so often and so loudly, that many of the rest of us just went along with it. We were afraid of looking prudish, rigid, old fashioned, or out of touch with "what was happening," as was often said. So we remained silent rather than risk being seen as judgmental or as extremists. Whether imposed by an individual or by a group, this kind of pressure is manipulation. Gradually, with so few people challenging this narcissistic notion, more and more of society accepted it as *a* truth.

As a result, we see an overabundance of Charmers and con artists today. It has become so acceptable that we are quite blasé about it, which allows more and more Charmers to develop and more and more people to be hurt by them.

Manipulation differs from motivation in that manipulation is totally for the benefit of the manipulator. To motivate someone is primarily for the recipient's benefit, although it may also benefit the one doing the motivating. The Charmer is so seductive that his manipulation always looks mutually beneficial, or it even may appear that he is working primarily for another person's benefit.

Since the Charmer is blind to the fact that he is a manipulator and blind to the realization that those in his path are being victimized, he sees his interaction with them as a win-win exchange. He even sees himself as giving more than he receives, since other people seek him out and they seem so happy after being with him.

His grandiosity makes him believe that he should be judged "differently." He should never have to stand in line like ordinary people.[2] (See the *Diagnostic and Statistical Manual of Mental Disorders, Fourth Edition*, pg. 358.) The Charmer is a narcissist, preoccupied with feelings of envy, and he reacts to criticism with feelings of rage, shame, or humiliation (even if not expressed). Depressed moods are extremely common. Personal deficits, defeats, or irresponsible behavior may be justified by rationalizing or lying.[3] (See *DSM*, Fourth Edition, pg. 359.)

It's the aftermath of the decades of the sixties and the seventies that reveals the truth. It's rarely detected by anyone who has not been victimized or who has not witnessed someone else's victimization. The Charmer is instinctively aware of how far he can go with a situation or a person. He won't use his skills full-strength on anyone but a captive audience, which usually includes family members, subordinates, a spouse, or someone with deep emotional ties to him—someone he believes would never have the courage or ability to walk away because of their love for him. He also doesn't hear or acknowledge what he doesn't want to deal with from them.

In his narcissism, he assumes those closest to him see him as just as deserving as he sees himself. Therefore, why would they be offended by being asked or expected to always respond in the way that is best for *him*. Basically, Charmers are users. Their needs are primitive survival hungers that have been submerged, disguised, and denied. Their wants are what they believe they need or should have.

Since Charmers are uncomfortable being alone, they need others. In groups, there are no demands or real tests for personal sincerity. The larger their audience, the easier it is for them to slip through the crowd and have no one really know them well. The larger their audience, the greater the opportunity to gain more admirers and, thus, more validation of themselves. In a crowd, they can spread themselves thin for a quick getaway if caught or found out.

If a Charmer loses a quality friend or lover—one who is healthy, one who recognizes the inconsistencies in the Charmer's life and refuses to settle for less than an equal, reciprocal relationship—the Charmer will then gravitate to a level of friends or to a romantic interest with whom he *can* be successful, individuals among whom he is sure he can be seen as a hero.

Having lost such a person, however, can frighten the Charmer, because his worthiness has been challenged, and he's lost control. He will either tell himself that that person was really not all that wonderful, or he will become obsessive in trying to restore that relationship, out of fear that the person is right. If he can't make that happen, he seeks to discredit the other person—to make them less than himself in order to continue feeling good about himself. If substance abuse or some other addiction is present, all his associates will be at his own level or below. He needs to believe he's acceptable to everyone and superior to his immediate circle. Torn between sincerity and inability to perform, Charmers fake the former to hide the latter.

He's intimidated by an intelligent, perceptive woman, though he may admire her and see her as validation of his idealized self. Even if she is deeply in love with him and committed to their relationship, he lives in constant fear of discovery. He knows he's a fake. He can't trust her love. He doesn't really trust anyone or anything completely, because he doesn't trust himself. He only trusts the facade he's created and the things he can control.

One of the things a Charmer unconsciously does is to test situations and people. He "pushes the envelope." Like someone with a gambling addiction, he has to find out his parameters or the breaking point. What looks like exciting risk-taking behaviors, is really his search for the maximum safe edge to which he can control.

While it is certainly possible to have a close friend of the opposite sex, the Charmer seeks opposite-gender friends who will adore him or perhaps have a romantic interest, even if he is not romantically interested in them.

The odds are very high that if he believes he is involved over his head in a relationship, he will unknowingly or unconsciously sabotage that relationship to get her ultimate rejection of him over with. That way he can feel justified to move on to a more successful project. Either that, or he will reject her first, so he can feel superior and in control.

Healthy love or friendship requires being trustworthy and being capable of trusting someone, of being vulnerable to them. Vulnerability is opening oneself to the possibility of being hurt. Our level of trust in others is directly related to our own trustworthiness.

CHARMER — **CON ARTIST**

Charmer	(shared traits)	Con Artist
Self-deluded		Knows what he's doing
Because he needs & deserves it	Entitlement	Because he wants it
Expression of his idealized self-image		Tools to get what he wants
	Personal traits	
	Good verbal & nonverbal communication skills	
Finds those who'll appreciate his specialness & adore him		Sees opportunities to get what he wants
	Charm & personal appeal	
	Conscience distortion	
Has underdeveloped, adolescent conscience; sees through grid of his own needs (amoral)		Knows right from wrong; but chooses to do wrong selectively (immoral)
	Sees trusting and / or naive people to charm	
To gain admiration, preference, "hero" image	Self-centered; uses others	To get what he wants—power or material gain
	Distorted empathy	
Limited; none at all if it interferes with his needs		Selective until it interferes with his wants, then he has none
	Lack of remorse	
Can "fake it" to himself & others if it helps his image		For anything he wants, he can "fake it".
	Lack of repentance	
Makes promises, but moves on before accountability		Moves on before he can be discovered
	Manipulative	
Unconscious, doesn't "get it"		Conscious, "gets it"; moves on before confrontation

HOW DID THEY
GET THAT WAY?

A M I LOVABLE?" That is the question with which all humanity struggles. A child needs loving caregivers who encourage, yet have reasonable expectations of him. The caregivers need to balance this with reasonable boundaries, which give a sense of structure and security to the child. The child will then grow up with self-confidence and a sense of well-being and competence in life. He will find comfort and peace in the world he creates for himself.

If he does not learn to trust the world in those first few years of life, it will be because he does not see his caregivers as being trustworthy or the world as being a safe place. He will be fearful and will be hurt often. Fear and hurt are the primary emotions behind anger. He may just become an aggressively angry person, passive-aggressively withdrawn, or if he has the tools, he may quickly learn to get what he wants by using his charm.

Anger is the unspoken, unrecognized core emotion of the Charmer. Most often, the Charmer isn't even aware of his anger, except in isolated moments of explosions that usually border on absolute rage, from which he can recover quickly to maintain his persona. In the absence of the tools Charmers possess, the angry person becomes abusive. The flip side of the Charmer is the abuser, as shown in some of the case studies that will follow.

In her book *Men Who Hate Women & The Women Who Love Them*, Dr. Susan Forward describes the point at which psychological abuse escalates to physical abuse. There is a final control device that demands, as proof of her love, that a woman give up those things that make her unique and that are an important part of who she is. These men hate women. They are misogynists who demand a partner narrow her world to keep the peace between them.[4]

As reprehensible as the abuser is, his behavior is at least a more honest response. Bruises, bleeding, or dying will be believed. When someone is openly abusive, you know, and others can witness you've been abused.

When a Charmer abuses, victims don't know they are bleeding internally until they are already in the process of dying. They are like the frog cooking in the beaker. In addition to the inner pain, victims lose confidence in themselves and are not able to recognize they are truly being hurt, much less know how to prevent it, stop it, or heal from it. Their subtle emotional death goes undetected, unaddressed, and therefore, unavenged.

The Charmer's inability to express his feelings openly (or his having shut down awareness of them for various reasons) makes it necessary for him to develop a coping mechanism: a false self, a mask, an image of an idealized self. The sense of being out of control—of being powerless in his own environment and being subject to others' whims and circumstances—becomes frightening to him. Thus, the denial begins and the use of anything available to regain equilibrium is set into motion. For the Charmer, that tool is mainly his personal appeal.

When a person cannot be honest with his feelings or be himself, his acting out is in extremes. Such polarization reflects the extent of the Charmer personality. Creation of an idealized self is perfectionistic thinking, which is the extreme side of taking responsibility onto oneself for making things happen, for keeping the world running smoothly, and for eliminating potential and actual problems. In an attempt to manage these things, manipulation becomes necessary. But it is always a treadmill of impossibility met by defeat, followed by greater effort, more impossibility and defeat, and on and on.

For the Charmer, another manifestation of an extreme response to the inability to be real about himself or his feelings may be to act out depravity. With this behavior, the Charmer says, in effect, "Things are out of control. I can't make them right, so I'll give up, not try, and let what will happen, happen." The unspoken message here is *Someone come rescue me and make everything all right*. It's a passive-aggressive way of shifting responsibility onto others, society, the situation, or whatever is available at the time. The subconscious thought is *I'm being abused, therefore I'm entitled to compensation for the injustices*.

Both ends of the spectrum of the Charmer's behavior are motivated by fear of inadequacy, of being out of control, of free-falling in a world he can't trust. He uses whatever resources are available to hold on, to balance, to feel secure. The Charmer becomes self-destructive because of the guilt he feels about the impossibility of performing perfectly and because of the shame he feels at the possibility of being seen as inept or hopeless, fearing that his ineptness is the reason he can't make everything right. Shame is a way to try to excuse himself from changing.

The Charmer acts out in one of two ways:

perfectionism = guilt
(inability to perform—*doing*)

= the need to hide
and develop a false image

depravity = shame
(inadequacy of who you are—*being*)

Most often there is a seesaw combination. Either he is on top of the world, surrounded by admirers who feed his need to feel in control of his environment, to have all the answers, to make things work, or he is privately tortured by fears of not being able to keep it going, feeling hurt that he even has to try and angry at himself and others who make it necessary.

The Charmer's personality has developed in one of two ways. The first possibility is that his was a limited response to a troubled childhood, which caused the development of unhealthy coping or survival techniques. In Susan Faludi's book *Stiffed: The Betrayal of the American Man*, she cites extensive research, stating the repeated lament of men whose fathers did not teach them the traditional values of true masculinity or lead them through the process of becoming a man. These boys were left to draw from images in the media and entertainment industries, leading to an emphasis on image rather than substance. Skills of providing and protecting, as well as confidence in themselves and their competency, gave way to an artificial manhood of machismo, bravado, and misogyny. No wonder they feel lost, cheated, and angry.[5]

If such a child was able to develop the skills and charisma for being a Charmer, this way of managing life became a very pleasant avenue for escape from his feelings of abandonment and neglect and all those other feelings associated with childhood fears. He could avoid a lot of yelling, screaming, and punishment. Plus, he could get special privileges.

Unfortunately, the things one does to make it through a troubled childhood generally become problematic in adulthood. Tools used as a temporary necessity in childhood must be put aside to make way for mature attitudes and behaviors when one has grown up and has come into possession of adult autonomy and power. Otherwise, the die is cast for recycling childhood fears. This will be followed by impulsive shortcut responses—perhaps impulsiveness and obsession—that prevent real intimacy in relationships.

In such cases, the emotional maturity of the individual becomes stalled in the time between childhood and adolescence. The physical and intellectual development will go on, but emotionally he is still a child. Now that the "child" is thrown into the adult world and must make it on his own, he must hide his childishness.

Problem-solving skills need to be learned to give confidence for finding reasonable avenues of negotiation, as opposed to a hard-line either/or position. If the Charmer believes that only one can win and one must lose, then to ensure his own survival, he learns to make others believe a lie regarding their own success, while he is the secret benefactor of the outcome.

The second way the Charmer's personality may develop (with or without a traumatic or chaotic childhood) is just by being spoiled—by the child's having a sense of his own specialness and entitlement, an idea bestowed and supported by his early caregivers. It's about attitude, not about how much money, love, or material wealth one has. The spoiled child does not learn (as one should in growing up and maturing) that his specialness is no greater than anyone else's. He doesn't see other individuals has as unique, unrepeatable miracles of

God, nor does he perceive the specialness others automatically have in the eyes of those who love them.

The difference between the Kennedy and Rockefeller families illustrates this point. Both families were wealthy, both in public service. The Kennedys used public service for self-aggrandizement, as a tool for power and fame. The Rockefellers entered public service as a means of giving back to a country that had blessed them. In each family, the attitude regarding personal responsibility had little to do with their money but everything to do with whether they believed they were entitled or blessed.

A spoiled child does not have healthy self-esteem. Rather, he lives with the conviction that his specialness is superior to anyone else's, having no sense of healthy shame or limitation on his behavior. He believes he is entitled to have what he wants in the world, no matter what. He is still in the mode of what John Bradshaw calls "His Majesty, the Baby."

A spoiled child is an insecure child. He's not sure what he can trust if everything is permissible and no one is in charge. The first time he "bangs his head against something" because he can't do or have it (which is inevitable), it will challenge his trust in himself and in his caregivers who previously had permitted it. Having no boundaries is a scary thing, especially for children. They thrive and learn to trust and grow by knowing the boundaries and knowing what comes next.

How fast would you drive across a bridge that had no side rails? You'd probably go very slowly, if you went at all. However, when you *have* driven across a bridge, you've probably never touched the side rails. But you know they are there, and that gives you a sense of direction and security. You know what you can count on for protection. It's the same with boundaries and guidelines. Rules and laws are not there to inhibit our freedom and pleasure of life, but they give us a sense of safety and, thus, freedom. They enhance the pleasures we can afford to have because they assure us that things are all right.

When that spoiled child discovers he has been given a false sense of security and reality about life, he's going to be angry. He's going to feel deceived and frightened. (This sets in motion the cycle of fear-hurt-anger in the child, and it also creates a sense of needing to seize control to protect himself.) He's probably also going to receive some hard knocks from the world. Actually, if he does, and if he figures out how to respond in a healthy way, it's his only hope for maturity.

If he's able to see the truth about boundaries, he may come to understand that his parents likely meant well—or even were misinformed—but that they don't have all the answers to life. If he can then incorporate truth into his life on his own, he is still free to love and honor his parents, but he will have to take full responsibility for learning about life somehow and somewhere else from that time on.

This is not an easy choice. He may not be able to figure out how to do that, how to manage that split in his thinking. If he's been taught to see things as black or white, he may not realize that two concepts can exist side by side. If the situation is heavily weighted on the caregivers' side—that is, if the caregivers have greater power or influence than the input coming from the outside and the child is unable to individuate (and that is the key)—it will be very hard to overcome black or white thinking.

If Mom and Dad rush in to cushion that reality experience, intervening when there would otherwise be natural consequences for the child's behavior, or if the child continues in his denial or if he refuses to integrate his new knowledge and awareness, he will be further confused and frustrated by the mixed messages he is receiving. He will then have two choices.

First, he can go on depending on his parents or surrogates to continue the farce for him, avoiding responsibilities any way possible. This will probably include running from accountability or resisting it with open defiance. Many such people occupy our prisons, while other such individuals, just hold prisoner the people in their lives through threat, intimidation, or manipulation.

Second, if the spoiled child has the attractiveness and/or the communication skills that he needs, he can learn very early to charm his way around the rules or any inconvenient stumbling blocks. In his mind he figures, *If it is easy enough, why deal with issues head on? Why give up my advantage when I can get what I want and look good at the same time?*

One of the truths a Charmer can never know is how to have peace of mind or true joy. The word *no* in any form becomes a personal threat. He has moments or periods of time during which he feels a great sense of accomplishment, often based in his secret delight in having gotten away with something again. He has exchanged joy (which is based on peace and contentment) for happiness (which depends on managing happenings). He has traded long-term life satisfaction for short-term highs.

Charmers do this all at a subconscious level. It looks and feels as though life works very well for them. They usually act very confident and happy-go-lucky. However, there are those Charmers who may be shy and self-effacing, silently inviting you to come rescue or take care of them, but this is more often the female Charmer. Charmers will use whichever tactic works best, often alternating between the two strategies, depending on how they size up the situation. What they have learned instinctively, they do automatically.

What a Charmer wants may not be anything more than to be well regarded, the center of attention, to feel good about himself, to get by the easiest way, to make a situation go his way, to gain power, control, fame, or fortune in a small or large dimension. None of these goals is wrong . . . until attempts to reach them comes at someone else's expense or is a substitute for dealing with real issues or real feelings.

A Charmer can rationalize or justify his behavior, having no recognition or remorse for the pain he causes others in achieving his goals. Even if he sees the pain he's caused, he will tell himself that his own pain would be greater if he didn't do this. While he thinks this way, certainly there will be no repentance, which would mean a change of heart, turning to a new direction, and not repeating the behaviors. He may, on occasion, express remorse; however, he has no intention of changing what works for him, even though he may sincerely feel sorry at the moment that he's hurt someone. Chances are higher that he is "like the thief who is not sorry he stole, but awfully sorry he got caught," which was how Rhett Butler assessed Scarlett O'Hara's behavior in *Gone with the Wind*.

The longer the Charmer is successful, the more entrenched he becomes in his ways, and the harder it is to recognize or reverse the patterns. Lying and deceiving become a necessary and important part of his operation. He gets to the point where he doesn't even see what he is saying and doing as deception; he's just "telling people what they want to hear."

Prince Charming is a kind, good, healthy, fully functioning adult with whom one can have a mutually wonderful relationship. The Little Prince, the Charmer, is a man-child (or woman-child) who is the center of a universe that all others may only visit.

In their book *Why Can't Men Open Up?* Steven Naifeh and Gregory White Smith say that Charmers range from the boy-who-never-grew-up, with his disarming smile and calculated naiveté, to the ones who are "lethal" in there ability to involve a woman totally. One woman in her study described it as the difference between a high school play and a Broadway show. A really great actor, which is what a real Don

Juan is, can make you forget he's acting. He makes *himself* forget. She went on to say that if he's good enough, most women don't want to know he's acting. They're eager to suspend their judgment. They'll suspend anything. He's that good.[6]

The authors state that the Charmer is a master of forms of openness and intimacy that have no substance. Charmers are dead inside. This most closed type of personality is that of the most insecure of closed men, and such men have a very fragile ego. Instead of concealing emotions they do have, they make a show of emotions they don't have.

A Charmer uses his skills to control others for personal advantage. These skills may be either verbal or nonverbal. In fact, most of our communicating is nonverbal, so it isn't a big or smooth vocabulary that matters. If the Charmer is personally attractive, his effectiveness is greatly enhanced. These are the tools he uses to make life work for him and to avoid being responsible. It all comes down to motive, goal, and distortion of integrity.

Charmers are not easy to detect right away. Often they start out in a relationship as just nice, appealing individuals. The point at which his level of comfort or security is threatened is the point at which the Charmer will surface and go into action.

For many reasons, a Charmer is more likely to be male than female. According to counseling psychologist Dr. William H. Jones, men are more aware of their own needs than women are. Men are also more aggressive than their female counterparts in getting their needs met, and they have less guilt about pursuing fulfillment of those needs.

Males are socialized to be more assertive and aggressive, and indeed, they are usually expected to be this way. This expectation creates in them a sense that whatever it takes to get what they need—or what they think they need (i.e., what they want)—is acceptable behavior.

Society is more tolerant of male behaviors. Men are more readily excused than females when they function impulsively.

Females tend to be caretakers of others first, and most of their socialization has been in that direction. Until the Women's Movement, it was less acceptable for women to explore their own needs, much less pursue getting them met. Women tend to put others before themselves; so it is still difficult for them to establish and pursue their own needs.

Society tells females it is not as acceptable for them to show anger or even to get angry. Anger in a male is seen as being assertive; in a woman, it is viewed as being aggressive or hysterical. That may explain why females are more prone to turn that anger inward and become depressed. Depression is much more common among females than among males.

One research cited that males are more likely to use their attractiveness to an advantage in the workplace. Females often struggle to be taken seriously. Certainly this does not mean that some women don't also use their feminine wiles to gain advantage. For most of history, it has seemed to be their only leverage. It has been a game that both parties knew was being played, a game to which both silently agreed. However, with recent legislation, opportunity, and consciousness-raising, most women are anxious to compete head-to-head.

Another research stated that attractiveness in a woman may now work against her in business. Very attractive women are promoted less often than those moderately or less attractive, regardless of qualifications. There appears to be a backlash of fear on the part of management that they may appear to have promoted on the basis of a woman's sex appeal.

Another possible reason Charmers more often are male than female lies in the difference between the way the genders view power or control. Women are more likely to seek *equal* power: a 50/50 cooperation. Men are more likely to a view 50/50 arrangement as having no control or power at all. For example, the athletic event that ends in a tie is not welcomed enthusiastically. That's why such a thing as overtime has been created; someone has to win by at least one point. A 51/49 ratio of power is the least acceptable. And the "teamwork" that men are supposedly better at than women exists only if the team wins and each player individually shares in the glory of being a winner.

The obsessive-compulsive component that drives the substance abuser to resort to his or her behaviors is the same as the motivation for Charmers in their need for confirmation of their ability to be in control of life and to be lovable.

Charmers are most likely to be a youngest son, a favored one, or the only male in a family. A youngest daughter is not as likely as a youngest son to be a Charmer. Not every family has a Charmer. A family can have more than one Charmer, such as the Kennedy family, in which all the males were Charmers, beginning with the father, who was a very strong role model to his children.

In a review of the book *President Kennedy: Profile of Power* by Richard Reeves, Mel Small of the *Detroit Free Press*, states, "He [Reeves] does, however, offer a fast-paced, fascinating, and often thrilling narrative of crisis after crisis. . . . An impatient, easily bored man with a short attention span, Kennedy thrived on those crises, even though several nearly resulted in the Third World War. This pragmatic 'managerial politician' craved action and apparently sought danger."[7]

As John F. Kennedy seduced the nation and then the world, he brought a "high" of optimism and euphoria, which some compared to the mythical state of Camelot. With his death, that same body of hero worshipers, in their grieving, threw themselves into "dropping out and turning on." This sent things in the late 1960s into a tailspin; the mindset of the world changed, and people began to question everything in which they had once believed. The residue of that time has, like dust, settled onto our society. Recollecting ourselves and our values has been like dusting each and every piece of our fabric, an endless, painstaking task that goes on and on.

Normal, healthy grieving is for a season, ultimately resolving into acceptance and going on with life. It maintains appreciation for that which is lost but gradually separates it from the reality of the need for life to go on. Some of Kennedy's most ardent admirers would compare him with Abraham Lincoln. However, after Lincoln's death, although the nation grieved and was temporarily stunned, a collective "level head" returned, leaving society's fabric intact. In retrospect we see that, as a nation, we had a healthy, objective love for Lincoln but a very codependent fantasy attachment to Kennedy.

"Youngests often spend much of their lives trying to make a significant contribution to earn respect. . . . They generally strive to be independent and love to turn things upside down, so they're more likely to become entrepreneurs, researchers, writers, artists, or activists. . . . Saddled with built-in inferiority complexes, they tend to resent people who help them, interpreting the help as a signal that they aren't trusted to do well on their own. Though some youngests may mask their insecurity as bravado, others make the mistake of relying on charm and assuming their sins will be easily forgiven."[8]

Explaining how someone becomes a Charmer is to try to understand them and their effect on us and everything in their world. At the same time, it is knowing reasons are never excuses. We all make choices. Some of us have harder choices to make than others, but we are still responsible for the choices we make. Understanding can show us where to begin to correct a situation or to help another person to see and begin to help themselves. Understanding does not remedy anything. It is the key to open the door, but one must choose to walk through that door.

The Role of Alcoholism/Addictions

The description of a Charmer is similar to that of an alcoholic or drug user. Most alcoholics or drug addicts are Charmers or con artists, because lying and secrecy are vital parts of hiding and sustaining their habit. For both, their lives are based on self-delusion. It's often difficult to tell which comes first: the alcohol or the Charmer's personality. Alcohol encourages Charmer-type behavior, and the Charmer is easily drawn to alcohol to facilitate his lifestyle, as well as to help numb the pain of his existence. Once again, we see this behavior being used as a coping or survival technique.

THE FLIP SIDE:
ABUSERS

A GREAT DEAL has been written, published, heard, and seen in the media regarding domestic violence, including spouse and child abuse, as well as about the general increase in society's violence. Some argue that there is no more violence today than in past eras. These individuals say we are just more aware of abuse and violence because of mass communication and because people feel more comfortable exposing it. Yet there are many studies revealing that, although those two arguments have some validity, there truly is more violence today than in the past.

While we may believe we are, indeed, more enlightened to-day, there is another ingredient that perhaps explains why violence may have increased, and that ingredient is our greater expectations. We are surrounded by advertising and bombarded with airbrushed images of what is possible for us, and the level of our exposure to these suggestions tends to make us see them not merely as what *could* be, but as what *should* be and what should be available to each of us. Instead of the declaration of the right to freedom to *pursue* happiness, we begin to interpret that right as everyone's entitlement to or guarantee of happiness, whatever we decide it takes to make us happy. And so happiness becomes not the American dream to be pursued, but the inalienable right of being an American. The mature individual understands the difference. The Charmer, con artist, and abuser, on the other hand, are all stuck in their childish expectation that their wants and needs are demands and rights to which they are entitled for no other reason than that they exist.

As stated earlier, when charm and personal appeal no longer work, and if the stakes are high enough, the Charmer will resort to intimidation, blaming, and abuse—whether verbal or emotional abuse and all the way to physical abuse and even murder. Remember, the Charmer is motivated by what he believes to be his needs for survival. He is only one frustration away from violence.

The con artist, whose goal is primarily material gain, can afford to back off, move on, or wait to replay his game in a more promising scenario. Only if he cannot escape, will he resort to attack. Since he is fully conscious of what his plan is and what he is doing at all times, he's very adept at not being around when discovered. His game is the scam, embezzlement, and fraud.

One type of abuser is the bully. He needs to be dealt with at an early age with appropriate consequences for his behavior. If not, he'll grow up continuing to be abusive. Unchecked, his behavior progresses to terrorism and violence. All abuse contains some element of stalking as one of the tools.

Stalkers are predators. They are obsessive. They want to be like their victim or to possess them, to make them part of themselves. It is not an issue of love but of control. They see their victim as more powerful than themselves and are attempting to take away that power and make it their own.

Stalking is an act of terrorism, which if not stopped, will progress to violence. It is insidious, leaving open-ended the questions of how far the stalker will go and of what lies ahead for the victim. While other forms of abuse may begin with threats and intimidation and escalate to criminal acts or pathological behaviors against another person, stalkers are pathological from the beginning. Their goal is to render their victim powerless beneath their fantasized superior power.

Stalkers are cowards. Their actions are covert because they realize if they were open in their activities, they would be seen as sick, pathological. They are usually from a very dysfunctional background and believe they are hopeless in climbing out of their lot in life. So they concoct a fantasy life where they live secretly.

Victims of stalking suffer emotional abuse, and they fear the possibility of unknown potential physical danger. They are revictimized again and again by disbelief or trivialization of their experience by others who cannot grasp the significance of their plight. Because of the lack of validation and the cunning of the stalker, victims often doubt their own perception and never feel truly safe again. Stalking is psychological robbery and emotional rape.

POWER AND CONTROL

PHYSICAL **VIOLENCE** SEXUAL

USING COERCION AND THREATS
Making and/or carrying out threats to do something to hurt her • threatening to leave her, to commit suicide, to report her to welfare • making her drop charges • making her do illegal things.

USING INTIMIDATION
Making her afraid by using looks, actions, gestures • smashing things • destroying her property • abusing pets • displaying weapons.

USING EMOTIONAL ABUSE
Putting her down • making her feel bad about herself • calling her names • making her think she's crazy • playing mind games • humiliating her • making her feel guilty.

USING ECONOMIC ABUSE
Preventing her from getting or keeping a job • making her ask for money • giving her an allowance • taking her money • not letting her know about or have access to family income.

USING ISOLATION
Controlling what she does, who she sees and talks to, what she reads, where she goes • limiting her outside involvement • using jealousy to justify actions.

USING MALE PRIVILEGE
Treating her like a servant • making all the big decisions • acting like the "master of the castle" • being the one to define men's and women's roles

USING CHILDREN
Making her feel guilty about the children • using the children to relay messages • using visitation to harass her • threatening to take the children away.

MINIMIZING, DENYING AND BLAMING
Making light of the abuse and not taking her concerns about it seriously • saying the abuse didn't happen • shifting responsibility for abusive behavior • saying she caused it.

PHYSICAL **VIOLENCE** SEXUAL

DOMESTIC ABUSE INTERVENTION PROJECT
202 East Superior Streat
Duluth, Minnesota 55802
218-722-2781

WHERE CHARMERS
ARE FOUND

B Y NOW IF YOU have recognized Charmers whom you know, you realize they can be found anywhere. Some professions seem to draw Charmers because of the skills of persuasion they possess. At the same time, Charmers are drawn to certain fields that best present opportunities for them to act out these skills: law, politics, sales, entertainment, media, business, etc. (Again, this does not mean that all skilled people in these professions are Charmers.) A Charmer can just as well be found working on an assembly line or as a repair person.

Regardless of the job, a Charmer will be a Charmer. In fact, some Charmers may even gravitate toward an area one might least expect, because in that place, they find opportunities to shine that much brighter. In any case, it will almost always be a job in which they are heavily involved with people.

Think about some of the service fields—especially education and even the church—places we expect altruism and selflessness. What better hideouts for a Charmer to function unsuspected? And what better place than the church to expect and extract repeated forgiveness and tolerance?

Since Charmers have short-lived relationships, many are likely to be single, frequenting bars and other hangouts. A recent phenomenon is singles organizations, including many in churches. It doesn't matter what their job, they will act out their game in some area of their lives.

PART TWO

CASES AND PROFILES

Typical Charmers:
Classic Examples

Scarlett O'Hara

PROBABLY THE CLASSIC female Charmer is the fictional character Scarlett O'Hara in *Gone with the Wind*. The author, Margaret Mitchell, made the motivations and inner workings of Scarlett's mind open to us, the audience, not only in the book but also in the movie. We could hear and see her thought process, her rationale, her plotting. We could see that she was aware at all times of her abilities to charm people, but she saw no connection between using her charms for her own ends and the effect that doing so had on others and on her relationships with them. She felt perfectly justified in doing whatever it took to get what she wanted. She told herself it was right.

From the beginning of the movie, it was apparent there were those who were wise to Scarlett and her excessive use of her feminine wiles. Viewers weren't sure at that point, however, that accusations were not just jealousy on the part of less attractive and less charming females. The only female who seemed oblivious to the truth about Scarlett was the ever codependent, Melanie.

The males all seemed to delight in their captivation by Miss Scarlett—all except that charming rogue, Rhett Butler. He seemed to be the only male who could see the truth about her. In spite of what he saw, Rhett was attracted to her. He found himself fascinated by a woman who was straightforward enough to aggressively pursue what she wanted. There was a level of honesty in that to him, but he was the only one able to see it that way. He recognized and admired it because of his own cunning abilities. He knew he would be playing with fire in a relationship with her, but he felt pretty confident of his own ability to fight her fire with his own.

Even the clever Rhett Butler would eventually be conquered and undone by Scarlett. She would prove to be too much even for him. He continued to underestimate her. In the end, the only thing left for him to do, if he hoped to salvage his own life and have any kind of a healthy future, was to leave her.

Any of the men in Scarlett's life would have been horrified instead of charmed if they had known what she was all about. But rather than see Scarlett as the self-serving woman she was, it was easier for these men either to deny the truth about her to themselves (as Scarlett's father, Gerald, and the virtuous Ashley did) or just to be oblivious like all the others. Protocol for Southern gentility in that particular time and setting would not allow for such an open truth. Therefore, it was easier to ignore or deny the reality about Scarlett than to have to deal with it.

With Rhett, the attraction wasn't just that he and Scarlett were alike. They weren't. There were similarities in their knowledge of people and in their maneuvering. Rhett was very charming. He could even con people on occasion, if he chose to, but basically he was honest. He enjoyed his cavalier image, which challenged the lofty social attitudes and practices of the day. Rhett was captivated by Scarlett's excitement, recklessness, and singleness of purpose. He admired her breaking from the establishment of the day, while with such skill, staying within its parameters.

Scarlett's years of longing for the elusive yet noble Mr. Wilkes is a characteristic of the Charmer's fixation on a challenge she or he is afraid can't quite be met. This challenge and its accompanying fear creates a drive that takes on great intensity. The Charmer, Scarlett in this case, *must* then meet that challenge to feel secure of her own power in her world. Her obsession with Ashley blocked any availability to any other man or relationship.

Profile

Katy Scarlett, as her father affectionately called her, was the eldest of three daughters but clearly the favorite of her father, Gerald O'Hara. She grew up as a caricature of the exaggerated grandiosity of the South before the Civil War. Her beauty, wit, and charm captivated every male she met. Only the most brutally honest of her female acquaintances would dare call attention to her misuse of her assets. Even then, propriety prevented exposing her. The others were simply too gracious to notice or to believe what they saw happening.

More than a "steel magnolia" as so many Southern women are, Scarlett was more like a velvet hammer in getting her needs met. She told herself that she wasn't hurting anyone, that her needs were real, and that pursuing them aggressively was reasonable. She even saw her actions as honorable: for instance, her dancing with Rhett in order to secure his financial contribution to the "cause" of the South, though she still was in mourning for the death of her husband.

Scarlett's response to the war and to the upheaval it caused in her life, prevented her from growing out of her adolescent narcissism. The traumatic events in her life pushed her to rely on whatever skills she possessed merely to survive and protect her family, while also trying to preserve the fairy-tale life she had loved. She was prematurely thrust into the parental role of providing for her younger sisters; her demented father; the helpless Melanie and her baby; and the defeated, discouraged Ashley. At the same time, she was desperately trying to find a way to prevent the loss of her precious Tara—the only semblance of identity she had and the only thing giving her the ability to go on. This could have been a time of redemption for her, a process of maturing, had she allowed it, but she remained self-absorbed.

In her mind, whatever she had to do to make life work for her was justified, whether it was marrying her sister's fiancée (thinking she could handle, better than her sister could, his money-making skills for the benefit of her own goals) or dressing in her mother's draperies to charm the condemned Rhett Butler out of his money before he was hanged.

When the war ended, survival was no longer the issue. Now she needed to gather as much material resources as she could to feel safe, to feel secure against ever feeling that vulnerable again. She had a deep need to gather more wealth, justifying it along the way (as she did with Ashley) in using "free darkies" at reduced wages in her mill. She kept Ashley weak and close by, keeping him working for her. If she couldn't have him as her husband, she would do the next best thing: keep him near. In doing so, she hurt everyone around her who loved her. She refused to see what she was doing to them, even when they spelled it out to her.

She saw what she had done only when she began losing the things that did matter to her: her daughter, Bonnie; the unborn baby she secretly hoped would bring her closer to her husband again; Melanie; her dream of Ashley (a dream on which she had wasted her life); and Rhett, who gave up on her in the end.

But she just couldn't reform. To keep from seeing the reality of the life she had created in her self-centeredness, she immediately escaped by clinging to what had worked for her in the past: Tara, which symbolized her old life and power. It strengthened her confidence in herself that she could somehow come up with a plan to undo all that had happened, to blot out the pain, and to make life work for her again. She would think about that tomorrow.

Insights

The Charmer sees all of life according to its impact on her personally. She is preoccupied with finding ways to feel good about herself and to feel safe.

The Charmer is often girlish/boyish to illicit from others all the warm, nurturing feelings people enjoy exhibiting toward children.

Charmers are seductive, serious flirts, whether it is obvious or subtle.

The Charmer will not change as long as her life works for her and as long as there is any means to escape facing the reality of her pain and the consequences of her choices. Charmers don't hear what they don't want to hear, or see what they don't want to see, or understand what they don't want to understand. To acknowledge truth would mean having to respond and change.

At points of intervention, if the Charmer just doesn't "get it," she continues in her own little world of self-destruction and hurting others.

Charmers make commitments or promises, but they follow-through only on the ones from which they get the most personal-benefit mileage or the ones they can't avoid. They really mean to commit, but don't have the healthy ego-strength to sustain reciprocal relationships.

Hal

"I've always been able to get people to do pretty much what I want them to do," Hal said matter-of-factly as he sat in the marriage counselor's office. He was thinking of how surprised people would be to know that he was failing at his third marriage. He was so successful in everything else and was such a fun person to be with. He was Mr. Personality, a born salesman, a walking party. He was personable, attractive, yet self-effacing. What a guy! He was a great storyteller and had an infectious laugh that, on its own, caused others to laugh too.

One of his clients once made a powerful statement to him: "Salesmen spend time with us to get our business. We give you business to get *you* to spend time with us." Hal was included in private gatherings of clients—gatherings that were usually reserved for family only. He was asked to be in their weddings, to be godparent to their children. Some put their jobs on the line to give him business. His clients wined him, dined him, and gave him gifts, which is the opposite of how it's supposed to go in sales. But why wouldn't they? He was not just someone they did business with; he was their friend.

Hal once remarked to his wife about how many people considered him their best friend and how surprised they'd be to know he hardly thought of any of them at all when they weren't around. It seemed to escape them that they did all the calling, that he never called them. Even when invited to their homes for strictly social events or for a weekend visit with them or on joint vacations, Hal reminded his wife, "We're still working." However, in spite of the fact that the relationships with his client-friends weren't truly reciprocal, Hal seemed to need their attention. In fact, he craved it, and he always knew how to get it too. It was a gift he had.

Yet Hal's personal life was crumbling, again. His wife and children saw another side of him—the real side. He was a man of great personal doubt and a growing insincerity, a man with many fears, much anger, and great resentment. He often would come home, joking about having to "glint" all day, and would bare all his teeth in a fake smile. He would complain of feeling like a vending machine, everyone was always wanting something out of him.

He often said he felt as though he prostituted himself for business, and he did. Hal violated his own values to gain and keep clients. He would drink excessively, go along with dishonest or immoral actions, and even arrange call girls for some clients. At times he even prostituted his family by using their home as a bar and restaurant to impress clients. His career came before the sanctity of his home. At such times and in such circumstances, he called his actions "situation ethics."

To those closest to him (those who loved him and whom he said he loved), Hal had difficulty giving just himself, just his love and commitment. It was hard for him to trust their love, and he did not feel worthy of it unless he somehow earned it or had manipulated for it. He had grown so used to love costing him something, that he had a hard time accepting unconditional love. When he tried to trust it, he went too far, repeatedly testing it with unacceptable behavior. In his mind, if they didn't unconditionally accept whatever he did as being okay, they didn't really love him. He believed that unconditional love meant unconditional acceptance of all his behaviors, good or bad.

Hal even began viewing his current family (as well as his two former wives and the children he'd had with them) as only taking from him, valuing him only for his increasing success and the easy lifestyle it bought. The truth was that they had loved him when he'd had nothing, before the easy money had come and, indeed, in spite of what it had done to cloud his vision and distort his values. They wanted *him*, his *time*, not just the things he was able to buy for them. The children actually abhorred money beyond what was required for a reasonable, comfortable living. To them, money symbolized the ax that had destroyed their family.

To Hal's wife, family relationships and meaningful friendships were more important than building a bank account or a business. Her circle of friends and activities, however, had shrunk to include only those people who were clients or who could further Hal's career. There never seemed to be time for their other friends, especially hers. Hal had become a human "doing" rather than a human being.

In addition, Hal's social drinking had escalated into functional alcoholism. He still did his job well, but his relationships were deteriorating. It was hard to know if the pressures of his growing success and the guilt he felt over his eroding integrity caused him to drink more, or whether his steady course toward alcoholism was causing him to avoid confrontation from loved ones and to seek refuge in work and superficial relationships. His drinking was so well managed to protect his image, that only his wife even saw it as part of the mix of their problems.

Hal's wife acted as the peacemaker among everyone, even in their relationships with his ex-wives and his children. However, her attempts to keep their collective feet on the ground were rebuffed and resented by Hal, and he regarded her efforts as holding him back. When finally he left her and the children, he said, "I refuse to be accountable to anyone for anything. I don't feel so guilty when I'm not around you."

The marriage ended. The marriage counselor described Hal as a loner, capable of loving only so much. The only comfort Hal's wife felt was from the counselor's statement to her: "Whatever he had to give, you got it all." Hal had left a trail of devastation for his family somehow to make sense of, grieve, clean up, and adjust their lives to.

Although leaving his family had been his choice, Hal again felt rejected and abandoned. No one knew, however, if he even would grieve losing his wife and children. Chances are, he would try to fill the void of their absence with more distractions, such as work, fun, toys, alcohol, fast living, and superficial relationships that offered a demand-free means of receiving more adoration. Hal had always said that when a situation got uncomfortable for him, he would pull the old "ostrich trick": He would put his head in the sand and pretend the problem wasn't there. He was proficient at avoiding reality. He knew how to live in denial, and so, if he chose not to, he would never have to grieve the loss of his family or feel the pain of their absence.

Many people who knew Hal, remarked admiringly about the reckless abandon with which he approached life, grabbing all its gusto. Hal played hard, and for him, life was one big party. His ready sense of humor and ability to see fun in most situations were only a thin disguise covering a seething anger just below the surface. This hostile side frequently surfaced in sarcasim veiled by a kind of innocence and little-boy charm.

If ever confronted on any of his behavior, he'd offer a sincere apology and then laugh about it behind the backs of those to whom he had apologized. If confronted on anything, he'd respond in one of two ways: (1) he'd explode in anger and defensiveness, withdrawing in prolonged silence and indifference; or (2) he would dismiss the importance of the issue and pre-excuse himself by saying, "All right, I'm sorry; I made a mistake, and I'll probably go on making them," as if this made everything all right.

He was talented and charming, yet privately he was insecure about his worth, about his being lovable, and even about his sexual preference. He stated privately to his wife several times that he had a bad self-image. He was disappointed about not being a good athlete in any sport, so he had become a "clown," going for the laughs rather than proficiency on the playing field. But his insecurity always remained. "If people really knew me without my happy-go-lucky mask, they wouldn't like me," he once offered.

Another time, he said, "I've never been very secure with women. I need someone who's submissive and vulnerable." Indeed, when his drinking produced a Dr. Jeckyll-and-Mr. Hyde personality in him (and his behavior became more bizarre, inconsistent, and offensive), he became threatened by the healthy responses and boundaries of those around him, particularly those of his wife. He then turned his attention primarily to their eldest daughter, looking to her as an ally, and surrogate wife in every way but sexually. This amounted to emotional incest for the daughter, which later caused emotional stress for all the family members.

On more than one occasion he said self-effacingly, "I really believe my secretary (also several other female clients and acquaintances) is legitimately in love with me."

A complex, paradoxical man, a hurting, angry, empty man. Like a guest of honor at a banquet who cannot bring himself to receive the gifts he's offered and who hungers while surrounded by sumptuous food, Hal longs for intimacy in a room of potential friends and lovers who remain strangers to him.

"What a guy!" people admiringly say of him, not knowing his private hell. "A prince of a guy!"

He's a Charmer.

Profile

Hal was the baby of a family of four children, the only surviving male. An older brother, the firstborn, had died in childhood. Hal was his mother's "blue-eyed boy" and was the only living male she really loved. The tragic death of her oldest son caused her to hover and cling protectively to Hal.

Hal's mother had been abandoned by her own father when her mother had died during childbirth. After seven years, her father returned and took her and her younger sister from the grandmother with whom they'd lived and whom they loved. Her father subjected her to several short-stay stepmothers, and she developed deep resentment toward him.

Hal's father was a loosely responsible, fun-loving vagabond who had moved his young family to an isolated part of Texas. As a means of coping with his eldest son's death, Hal's father made a silent emotional retreat and remained relatively uninvolved in the family's life, especially in his son's. He worked away from home most of the time, giving Hal's mother further feelings of abandonment and anger.

Hal was used by his mother as a surrogate replacement for every male in her life who had disappointed her. With an absentee father, there was no man around to offset or counter Hal's mother's complaints about the men in her life. How was Hal to feel good about being male? How was he to feel free to love the men in his life, such as his father and grandfather, whom he adored but whom his mother resented? Hal's perceived message from his mother was that he could not love her and, at the same time, love the men who had abandoned her.

Hal's mother was an angry woman with a negative disposition. Hal grew up hearing a stream of disparaging remarks about men and about her distaste for sex. As a result, he grew to love, pity, and hate his mother and, subsequently, had similar feelings toward all other women in his life. His conflicting feelings made him fear a woman's possible power over him, and he resisted real, lasting intimacy with any woman. Hal was also torn between loyalties associated with his manhood and protection of his mother and loyalties associated with love for his father and grandfather. He developed an intense need to be around men.

Hal was the last male to carry on his family's name. His father had his heart set on Hal's becoming a minister in their denomination and told him so repeatedly. Hal was the whole family's pride and joy. He learned to use his ready smile and humor to get himself out of sticky situations and to get away from things he didn't want to face. Humor in this household was often used to escape acknowledgment of and to avoid dealing with issues and problems. Humor was also often used at another person's expense, in an attempt to boost one's own self-esteem. Feelings of any depth were never shared openly or discussed.

Hal was the only child to be sent to college. On him hung the hopes for success—success that no one else in the family had achieved. The family was poor, and Hal found this fact humiliating. Paradoxically, they were rather snobbish—a cover-up often used to hide shame and fear of inadequacy. They believed they were out of place in the rural, hick setting they had to endure. They disliked being surrounded by all those "holy rollers," which to them was anyone who was not in their denomination. They considered their church elite, and their association with it became their primary identity.

In this family, drinking was a right of passage into manhood, an escape into which Hal plunged for relief from the stress of being pulled in so many directions at such a young age. It became his haven as the years and pressures of adulthood mounted.

Hal was sensitive and intuitive, and his people skills were well developed. This combination made him an outstanding school counselor and had won him numerous awards. However, when the lure of an easier and bigger lifestyle appeared, the shame of his humble beginnings and the chance to shine for (and to) his family propelled him toward that new possibility. The intrinsic joy of nurturing and guiding troubled children was overshadowed by the open-ended opportunities for money as a salesman.

The family's pride was clearly visible. Hal was the hero his dad wasn't able to be. Hal worked in an office; Hal's dad had worked in the oil fields. The more successful Hal became in the business world, the more he realized the cost to his personal integrity and the more he feared his success truly diminished his father. It wasn't until his father's death that he became aware of the deep pain his "passing up Dad to make Mom proud" had caused him.

The American tradition of each generation bettering the last one was an external achievement only. Hal, however, had sold himself to appease his mother's need for a male hero in her life, at the expense of the dad who was a relative stranger to Hal. Hal saw his father as a misunderstood, unhappy man who misunderstood his family's needs and made them unhappy too.

Hal felt a lot of pressure. He tried to cajole and console his mother, but eventually it became difficult for him even to be in the same room with her for more than an hour at a time because of his impatience with and resentment toward her. He knew how unhappy his father had been in his marriage. He tried to win the attention and approval of his dad, while also trying to make his parents proud of his success. Hal felt the weight of being the standard-bearer for the whole family. If he couldn't be a minister, as his father had wanted, he'd at least be a church officer and Sunday-school teacher like his dad.

Hal took all his unfinished business with his family of origin into his marriages. When the usual marital difficulties took place, there was an inner nudge to not get trapped for a lifetime the way his poor dad had. Any autonomy or assertiveness on the part of Hal's wife brought memories of the angry, blaming, shrew Hal recalled from childhood memories of his mother.

He was not free to be and do what his natural inclinations told him, so he traded in his wonderful personhood to fill the role of caretaker of his family and their wants. He sold his gentle, aesthetic self to attain the status and money his family had been ashamed of not having.

Whatever he couldn't or wouldn't do, he'd joke about as unimportant anyway. What he did accomplish, he made sure others found out about it and praised him publicly for it, although it always appeared he was trying to ignore it or play it down.

Keenly aware of his assigned role as family champion, he became frightened and insecure about doing what he wanted in life. He lacked confidence that he could stand up to his family's expectations. The drinking was a comfortable escape from that anxiety and also from his repeatedly expressed fear of being a homosexual.

Hal's own time of rebellion against his family came with a brief marriage to a Mormon girl. He looked down on her religious background, and yet he felt inferior to her because of her family's wealth. He was disappointed at not being included in the family business. Her family lived comfortably while he struggled on a small teacher's salary. His limited input into the relationship and his condescending attitude that covered his sense of inadequacy led to the demise of the marriage. After this experience, he was back in his own family fold even more securely.

Hal's second marriage lasted only six months, just long enough to provide a name for the child he had fathered during a brief affair.

Hal's third marriage was at least to a Protestant, which satisfied his family. Even though she was one of those "holy rollers" of whom they had always made fun, she was a woman he and his family respected, one with whom he finally felt safe and loved for just being himself. However, he was never really able to detach from the unresolved issues with his family. Any ways of life or traditions Hal and his wife and children established as a family, that did not fit with his parents' traditions, were frowned upon. Eventually, that pressure plus his advancing alcoholism and workaholism, led him to cast aside his third family.

Hal has become financially successful. It's less demanding to love from a distance, so he has become a paternal figure who provides generously for his employees, his parents, and his extended family members—all except for his own children, whom he does not see anymore. They have become disillusioned by what his "success" has cost them and by the changes it has brought about in their father, turning him into someone they no longer know.

Hal would not allow his children their hurt or anger about his leaving, because it made him uncomfortable, so he dismissed them. For him, they no longer existed. Anyone or anything in his life that would challenge him to act responsibly or to change, he perceived as a threat. Hal always saw *himself* as the victim, never those he hurt.

The blackouts of incidents and the massive denial of his problems caused by the alcohol had left Hal thinking everyone else had changed, that they had abandoned him and let him down. Hal believed they no longer loved him. What he didn't see was that all those close to him—those who loved him—had to keep silent about what they saw happening to him. Otherwise, they would be excluded from his life, as his wife and children had been. It hurt them to see what he was doing, but they didn't want to be banished.

Hal's inability to detach himself from his dysfunctional family of origin and from their expectations prevented his bonding sufficiently with his own family to be able to weather the ups and downs of life. Hal now races on a fast track of increasing wealth, running with a jet-set crowd that brags and flaunts its drugs and infidelity. His family of origin is scattered and dying one by one. There is no legacy to his success, nothing to leave behind except his name on a company and a building. He's on a treadmill of activity and diversion, racing numbly toward self-destruction in great style.

As long as he listens to the crowd cheering and admiring him, and as long as he believes the lies he tells and lives, he'll continue thinking he has it made.

INSIGHTS

The Charmer is often the victim of others' expectations. Alcohol and other addictions easily become a crutch or an escape from the pressure, setting up a cycle of denial, watering the seed of the Charmer.

The Charmer has learned to use the skills at his disposal for survival if there has been trauma or deprivation in the formative years. Or the Charmer has developed as a result of being spoiled, not having had consequences follow inappropriate behavior, since he's likely managed to escape consequences by using his charm.

The Charmer has little or no staying power in close relationships. He can seem very focused and committed initially, but this is short-lived.

It is easier to do grandiose things and look like a hero to a large audience than it is to stick to the day-to-day, work-it-out tasks of family stability.

The Charmer is magnanimous in giving as long as it is *his* choice and as long as he can look heroic, but if you assert your own rights or ask for a commitment from him, you'll quickly see his other side.

The Charmer has a great need for control. He is the center of his world. In fact, he must be the center of his world or the center of the world of whomever he allows to get close to him.

The Charmer is generally uncomfortable being around people who are honest or who see through him, unless he decides he wants to test his own abilities on them.

His refusal to address, deal with, or work through guilt, hurt, or shame leaves the Charmer with a deep sense of self-pity. It makes him more prone to midlife crisis, which is a reemergence of the adolescence he never really resolved.

SACRED CHARMERS:
EXAMPLES FROM THE CHURCH
AND HELPING-PROFESSIONS

U NFORTUNATELY, the past two decades have been a time of misconduct on the part of a number of trusted caregivers. Mental-health workers have been cited for having sex with their clients. Teachers and day-care workers are reported to have emotionally and physically abused those in their care. There have been the infamous Jims: Jim Jones, Jim Bakker, and Jimmy Swaggart. Priests, ministers, and church workers have beguiled communities and congregations, while drawing women and children into secret alliances involving sexual violation.

Of course, the media has had a field day, drawing attention to such individuals as if they are a statement of what these helping professions, the church, or God are all about. We can't blame the media for exposing wrong-doers, since they need to be exposed, to have their influence cut off, and to have their victims be freed from further exploitation. However, we can criticize the lack of balance in the media's reporting. Focusing on these scattered instances of abuse is not a fair representation of the church and the helping professions, for there are legions of good and godly men and women who are sacrificial in their work to help heal others and to extend the "milk of human kindness" to the world.

As for those who *have* been involved in abusing others in their role as a professional helper or minister, these are people who, for the most part, believe in their own sincerity and public image (at least in the beginning they did). They are people who became drunk with power. They were given too little accountability and too much opportunity for their actions. They went too far in the belief of their own invincibility, because no one stopped them in time.

Charmers usually are careful not to risk their overall success by overstaying their ability to succeed. But if a Charmer gets on a roll, he may ignore or allow that instinct to be overshadowed and thus may be discovered. It's fortunate for the public when this happens.

When the Charmer is discovered in his abuse, the public's natural response of outrage is coupled with cries of "Why didn't someone see this and stop it?" or "How did they let someone like that work for them?" The questions are legitimate. The answers are more difficult.

First, as we've looked at the ability the Charmer has to be a chameleon wherever he is and to instinctively know how to win the confidence of others, we can see how hard it is to detect him and to predict when and what he might do. Second, we often are reluctant to take action in a troubling situation until a concrete problem surfaces, afraid we'll be labeled a negative thinker, a tattletale, a witch-hunter, someone who has to be in control, someone who is vindictive, or even an abuser ourselves. There is always a fine line between being petty or a gossip, and being a responsible neighbor or citizen. There *is*, however, a difference between mere gossip and reporting a lion in the street!

While our fear is understandable and perhaps even based in a dangerous truth, when we do not speak up, we run the risk of giving silent consent or unknowing collusion to the Charmer's inappropriate behavior. While the best we can do on the preventive side is to be educated and alert so that we can take precautions, on the proactive side, we can resolve, at least, to deal with the Charmer's known violations.

In organizations, such as churches, that exist to help others, the opportunity for abuse without consequences is abundant. Often the heads of such organizations are naive and foolish in their trust. Without intending to, a church can facilitate the abuse of unsuspecting people. Church leaders can unknowingly provide the Charmer within their ranks a level of credibility he likely could not have anywhere else.

The Christian goal of wisdom and discernment was modeled by Jesus Himself, and we are admonished in Scripture to have the mind of Christ. While Jesus' gospel was open to all, He understood that there were some from whom He had to distance Himself, for he "knew what was in their hearts." Jesus realized that many people were not open to truth, that there were those who were bent on their own agenda. He did not assume that everyone He met was positively motivated. He did not naively treat them as He did His followers and others He knew to be open to truth. There *is* evil in the world. There *are* people who have allowed themselves to become evil.

It is important that any organization educate its staff to identify and deal with those who would use or abuse their organization. It is also the responsibility of leadership to adequately train both staff and congregation in issues, such as identification and confrontation of sexual harassment, awareness of gender bias and differences, conflict resolution, and legal and moral ramifications of what goes on in the operation.

Leaders must be on top of these issues, or else they put themselves and their organization in great danger of liability, public scrutiny and ridicule. In this litigious society, a story of abuse in a church is a probable powder keg. In a society in which the medium is the message, this makes for a great front-page story and for very bad public relations.

The Church should be leading the way when it comes to social issues, not reluctantly being dragged into them from the rear. If wishful thinking and a Pollyanna attitude worked, we could empty all the jails and do away with the court system. The answers to social problems, however, are not found in positive thinking, but in "truth thinking." Feelings are not a barometer of truth.

As radio talk show host Dr. Laura Schlessinger stated, "We have created a unique society in which those who do bad things are shown compassion and understanding, and those who point out the badness and expect consequences and justice are called judgmental and mean. I believe this attitude is pervasive because it provides a huge gray area in which people don't have to assume responsibility for their actions, and they are immune from annoying judgment."[9]

Organizations and professions must self-monitor and refuse to shield offenders. Negligence in this area has resulted in skyrocketing malpractice suits and insurance rates, to say nothing of the loss of credibility. Understandably, people are uncomfortable with crisis issues, particularly issues as subtle as these can be. Often, we'd rather not know about or even talk about them, because we might then have to take action and deal with problems related to them. And that's distasteful. It is easier to ignore or forget about an issue, hoping it will go away. But it doesn't. It just goes underground for a while, hurts more people, gives the perpetrator an increased sense of sanction and security in his behavior, and then in some cases, resurfaces in a way we can no longer ignore.

People have a right to feel safe, especially when providing help, protection, or safety is the purpose of the group or person to which they have turned. It is important that abusers not be protected at the expense of others.

Father Ralph

Probably the very best example of a truly unconscious Charmer in contemporary literature is the fictional priest Father Ralph De-Briccasart in *The Thornbirds* by Colleen McCullough. Father Ralph was the epitome of good looks and attractiveness, and he was the personification of highest virtue. He was caring and chaste, with just the right balance of righteous indignation against injustice. While he was as sincere as humanly possible, he was also self-deluded until the end of his life. His persona and behaviors toward others were noble, honorable, and good, except in one little corner of his life: Meggie.

Father Ralph burst onto the scene at an Australian ranch at about the same time the Cleary family arrived with a houseful of boys and one little girl, Meggie, who was then about eight years old. The handsome young priest was ramrod straight in his clerical functions, daily bringing the Eucharist to the wealthy grande dame, Mary Carson. She must have been a generous contributor to the church to merit daily service by her priest, who traveled the many miles required to reach her house.

Mary Carson had her own agenda for seducing Father Ralph, and she resented the time and attention he gave to little Meggie. Identifying the good priest's Achilles heel in his growing relationship with the child, she watched their devotion deepen through the years and plotted her revenge against Father Ralph's virtuous rejection of her. She wanted him to fall.

Leaving her estate to the Catholic Church, with Father Ralph as the administrator, Mary Carson bypassed her own family in the matter of inheritance. Then, by stipulating that the Cleary family members were to occupy the Drageeda Ranch as long as any Cleary lived, she effectively tied Father Ralph to his temptation for life.

The uncommon attachment between Meggie and Father Ralph was to meet a supreme challenge when the little girl became a beautiful, desirable young woman who had eyes only for her priest. She had always loved him. Any young man she might meet would pale by comparison to him as her standard. She was his forever from the moment they'd met.

Past his protests against her love and desire to marry him, he could not separate himself from her regardless of the miles he put between them. He was in and out of her life, holding on to her as the constant thread running through his existence.

His ambition to be the perfect priest propelled him upward in his career until he reached the Vatican. The pope under whom Father Ralph served, observed the hidden struggle in the soul of his assistant. "What hurts so deeply that one has to hide it so well?" he once asked Ralph.

Ralph sought finally to confront his inner turmoil by facing his fears with Meggie. When she hid from him and ran away, it was the moment of truth for Ralph. He pursued and conquered her, giving in to his own unrecognized romantic love for her. It never occurred to him that with their love affair, he might father a child with her. It was as if his being a priest could not possibly allow that to happen. He couldn't be that human.

After the affair, Father Ralph was able to go back to his life of work in the church. His ambition turned out to be greater than his love. He chose to see his giving up Meggie's love as his ultimate sacrifice to the church. What greater measure of his true devotion to God? Now he could feel worthy of being a priest and feel certain that he was giving his all to God.

For Meggie, she was torn between her resentment at being offered up as a sacrifice against her will and her beautiful, secret satisfaction at knowing that she would forever possess part Ralph, in spite of himself, in the child she was carrying.

Years later, when Father Ralph would visit them at Drageeda, he would not recognize her son, Dane, as his own. However, Father

Ralph and Dane were inexplicably drawn to each other. Dane was the pure version of Ralph.

In her lifetime, Meggie had suffered one loss after another. As a child, her father and two of her brothers died. She grew up with a melancholy mother, who was incapable of showing love to her. Meggie naively married an irresponsible husband who abandoned her and their daughter. Repeatedly, she experienced losing the man she loved, to a God she grew to resent. And finally, she was bereaved of her only son, the treasured keepsake of her relationship with an unrequited love.

Dane had become a priest, following in his dad's footsteps, though neither of them recognized it as such. Meggie had lost the man she loved to God, and now she was losing her beloved son to Him as well: first to the priesthood, which she hated, and then to death. "What a jealous, possessive God," she said. "He takes everyone I really love away from me."

But unlike Ralph, who sacrificed Meggie to God, Dane had sacrificed himself and his life while trying to save someone from drowning. His motives were that of a true priest and a noble human being. With Dane's death and the discovery that Dane was his own son, Ralph saw in Dane what he himself had always wanted to be and what, indeed, he had thought he was. But now Ralph realized that he had never been what he'd imagined. Through that discovery, he learned his own humanity and, finally, true humility. Through that discovery came his true salvation.

At the end of his life, Ralph acknowledged that his ambitions had not been motivated out of love for God as he had so frequently said but out of love for self. "I never made a choice for love—love of Meggie or of God—but for myself," he confessed just before his death.

"In spite of everything, in spite of all your losses," he said to Meggie, "you have always gone on loving." Ralph saw his own inadequacy in comparison to her integrity, realizing that she was closer to God than he was, that she loved as God loves, completely and unconditionally. He also came to realize that he could blame no one but himself for his mistakes.

As he was dying, Father Ralph told the story of the Thornbird—a bird that willingly pierces its own breast on a thorn believing that in its death, it will produce a beautiful song that will be worth it. "We know, but we do it anyway. We choose what we want, even knowing the cost," he concluded. Ralph realized his motive was for self, not God, but that was what he wanted, and it had not been worth the price he paid.

Profile

The author provides very little about Father Ralph's background. He appears in the story as full-grown and already a priest. He is recognized by everyone as a man who was sincere in his motives and his work. He is charming and attractive, liked by both men and women. This was evidenced in the passing of years in which everyone seemed to know about his relationship with Meggie, but they were content to ignore any ramifications.

His attractiveness is made obvious in the lust of Mary Carson—a woman old enough to be his mother or even grandmother. At parties, comments are always being made about what a shame it is that a man like Ralph has been wasted on being a priest.

The only thing Ralph ever mentions about his past is that his mother never forgave him for becoming a priest. However, it is never stated whether his mother's contempt for his chosen vocation was because her son would never be able to provide her with grandchildren, or because she resented that the priesthood took him away from her.

A "young prince" (a child who has everything going for him) is often synonymous with a blossoming Charmer (a child who is delightful to be around). If in Father Ralph's childhood, he was such a boy, it may have been difficult for his mother to lose him to the church. And if this was indeed the case, it is interesting that later in Ralph's life, this same scenario would present itself again in his relationship to Meggie. It becomes clear that, in his desire to demonstrate to himself and to God his devotion and his worthiness to be a priest, Father Ralph is willing to sacrifice the two women he loves most.

Many times in the story, throughout the years, Father Ralph reminds others that he is a priest. It often comes out almost in place of a real answer for whatever the issue being discussed happens to be. Ralph, however, remains totally oblivious to his pattern.

Father Ralph is quite unconscious of his need for admiration. Becoming a priest is the best way he can find to garner the various publics and the legions of admirers he enjoys. And he is accomplished at feigning a humility that feels real to him.

His obsession with Meggie is about feeling in control, not about loss. This obsession is made clear by the fact that he does not make peace early on with himself and with her where romantic feelings are involved. If he were not obsessed, he would not have continued to keep her dangling all of her life. He exploits her by allowing her to continue in her hope, love, and commitment to him, but he gives nothing back. Again and again, he offers her what his role as a priest demands, trying to nobly fight his love for her, never quite winning the battle.

In Meggie's inability to get beyond her romantic feelings, Father Ralph's appropriate response as an adult and spiritual leader should be to remove himself completely from her life, something he has opportunity to do. His actual response, however, is very seductive. It is the stuff of which fairy tales and romance novels are made. The only one who never sees this is Ralph himself. Meggie is seduced from childhood, so it becomes a way of life for her. She has no knowledge of her need to get over her feelings for Ralph nor of how to do so.

Under these circumstances, Ralph is assured of having a lifelong devotee in Meggie.

Father Ralph is a grown man when he meets Meggie, who is then a young child. Therefore, a reader who psychoanalyzes the story deeply enough, can make an argument for pedophilia on Father Ralph's part. At the very least, given his position as an authority figure, the kind of ongoing relationship he keeps with Meggie amounts to spiritual and emotional incest.

Throughout the story, Ralph chooses to live in denial. He demonstrates a need to cling to his idealized self-image, not acknowledging his real self with limitations and frailties. His denial goes on until the intervention of Dane's death. Only then does he realize his own delusion and the life he has stolen from Meggie and their child. In the end, this revelation of his selfishness at the expense of others and the pain and suffering he has caused, overcomes him, hastening his death.

Insights

Charmers who gravitate to positions designed to "do good for others" are really looking for a way to have more control over more people. For the Charmer, enough is never enough, whether it is admiration or control.

Charmers are unable to identify within themselves feelings of fear, mistrust, hurt, confusion. Since they are most comfortable living with a level of denial to avoid pain, it is difficult for them to have real empathy for others' feelings. They are emotionally distant and exhibit a pseudosensitivity.

Charmers will often neglect the needs of their own family or other responsibilities to go look like a hero to their other publics. They seek out situations in which they can look admirable without too much effort or cost to themselves. They have a grandiose sense of self-importance, which is disguised with a self-effacing humility.

Pastor Carlton

Deanna met with Pastor Carlton at the insistence of her husband, who was desperate for counseling that might save their young marriage. The disappointment this couple had experienced in their sex life was amplified by Deanna's postpartum depression following the birth of their first child. Deanna's husband was becoming increasingly impatient with his wife's lack of interest in physical intimacy.

Deanna was not happy about the idea of counseling, especially with a minister. She was already feeling inadequate and guilty. The last thing she wanted to hear was "You are not submissive enough." But Pastor Carlton didn't take that approach. Instead he told her, "When there are problems in a marriage, it is never just one person." From that point on, he began to reel her in. His gentle manner, his understanding eyes, and his sympathetic smile all eased her fears and apprehensions about trusting a man with her deepest secrets.

Deanna was an incest survivor. When she was twelve years old, her battering, alcoholic father exposed himself to her and began entering the bathroom regularly when she was bathing. He ordered her to not cover herself but to continue, and as she did, he made fun of her blossoming womanhood. Her mother, who was also verbally and physically abusive, did nothing to protect Deanna or her siblings.

Deanna was raped twice: once by a stranger and once by a family acquaintance. Her parents knew but did not pursue justice, nor did they seek counseling for Deanna. Their response was to refuse to discuss it, telling everyone who knew about it to put it out of their minds.

"I've learned that each of us has a 'BS detector,'" Deanna said. "When you go through abuse during your childhood, that detector is broken. So you do not know how to react when you are being violated, if you even realize it is a violation. You may feel shame, but you are confused. There is a reality testing of your judgment."

Just like father-daughter incest, professional incest, particularly with a member of the clergy, causes the victim to ask himself or herself, *Why would my pastor ask me to do something wrong?*

Eventually incest victims become so confused that they will conclude that there must be something wrong with themselves for thinking something is wrong with what is going on.

Pastor Carlton suggested to Deanna and her husband that he spend most of his time with Deanna, since she was the partner with sexual confusion and dysfunction in her past. The husband eagerly agreed. Once the couple started attending his church, the reverend was able to develop a friendly, personal relationship with the two of them. He included the husband in church lay positions and on committees of leadership, while inviting Deanna to help him in his office. The couple felt privileged and a part of Pastor Carlton's inner circle.

The pastor loaned the couple pornographic video tapes to help loosen them up in their lovemaking. He would occasionally call Deanna, asking her to respond to the tapes and to engage in phone sex, during which time he encouraged her to masturbate. This behavior progressed to his going to her house and watching the tape with her so she wouldn't be afraid or upset. He then would instruct her, step-by-step, in touching herself, trying to arouse her to orgasm while he watched and guided her. Pastor Carlton would also question the couple as to their sexual progress, doing so in such a way that they wanted to report favorably to please him. They didn't want to disappoint someone of his position who had taken such a personal interest in their problem.

After a year of counseling with Deanna, Pastor Carlton suggested that she attend a seminar on sexual abuse. He accompanied her for support. Ever so tentatively, he began crossing boundaries of her personal space. First, a reassuring touch of her hand. Later, a comforting arm around her shoulder. Then, massaging her back. And in their counseling sessions back at the church, the pastor began hugging Deanna before and at the end of each session. She noticed something different about the hugs, though. They just lasted too long, and the position and placement of hands and arms were not quite the same as with supportive, comforting, platonic hugs. It didn't feel right to Deanna, but she trusted him, so she said nothing and tried to put it out of her mind. During one hug, Deanna was sure the pastor had an erection, but she dismissed it as her imagination.

Deanna called the person who had conducted the sexual-abuse seminar to discuss her impression of what she was experiencing with her pastor, but she was told, "He's just helping you with transference." (*Transference* is a psychological term that means "working through feelings one has about someone else by projecting them onto a therapist or counselor.") Relieved, she took the seminar leader at his word, not realizing that he believed her concerns were a product of her imagination, since he did not think this famous pastor capable of impropriety.

During the next five years, Pastor Carlton groomed Deanna for his own sexual gratification. Little by little he convinced her that his inappropriate touches were for her good, that they were God's will, and that they would heal her of her past incest and sexual dysfunction. Whenever she questioned or withdrew from him, he would say, "You have been damaged so much, and when God wants to bless you, you cannot handle it."

Deanna was an aspiring writer. Because of Pastor Carlton's reputation as a preacher and his success in building a sizable church, he was able to made successful contacts so that she could be published. Her faith and confidence in him grew and grew. This man had only her best interest at heart. During one fondling episode, Deanna became upset. The pastor stood back, looked at her with disbelief, and said, "I just want to bless you any way I can; if it means helping you develop your talents, or touching you this way to help you learn to receive love, I want to bless you!" In this way, He normalized his abusive behavior. Once again, because he was her pastor, she believed him. Once again, she doubted her "BS detector," asking herself, *Why am I doubting God's man?*

Deanna and her husband had come to Pastor Carlton for help. Through therapeutic deception, the pastor told them he was healing Deanna. He told her he had to help her reenact the trauma she had experienced, so that she could expunge it from her life, breaking the spell of her father's abuse and replacing it with good, healthy attitudes toward sex and intimacy. He was to be a surrogate instrument through which she could relearn and then transfer all of it to her relationship with her husband.

After a period of slowly winning Deanna's complete trust and becoming that loving father-image she unconsciously sought, Pastor Carlton forged ahead into new territory. One day he told her to look at his genitals, and then, quoting scripture to justify his behavior, he went on to have her touch him. The moment she did, he ejaculated. She was immediately jolted into reality and felt horrified.

As she began waking from her nightmare, Deanna discovered she was not the only sheep being fleeced. Another one of the office workers (one to whom Pastor Carlton also had been inappropriately attentive), was aware of Pastor Carlton's interest in Deanna and had begun taping their phone conversations. This woman had shared the content of the tapes with Mrs. Carlton, who previously had been through this with her husband, but who determined that she was better off with him than without him. So Mrs. Carlton lived a life of feigned ignorance and would defend her husband to anyone who questioned her.

It is not unusual when multiple victims are involved, as they were with Pastor Carlton, for one victim to turn on other victims. Mysteriously, Deanna's car was vandalized, she began getting weird phone calls at all hours of the night, and a number of other unusual things began happening on a regular basis. Members of the congregation who had been her friends and admirers of her work suddenly became cool toward her. Many were condescending in their attitudes and treated her disrespectfully. She also sensed she was being watched and followed, and some people now had very private information about her that could only be gotten through reading her mail, checking up on her, and other such violations of her privacy.

Deanna had come to her senses, but she hadn't done anything about it yet. She was still reeling from the blows of reality. It wasn't long, however, before she and her husband were called before the elders, accused of "sowing seeds of discord among the brethren," and asked to leave the church. By this time, Deanna and her husband began sharing information about what had been going on. They now felt compelled, in their own defense, to tell the church leaders what they had experienced. Their account was not believed. They were stricken from the membership rolls and told that if they did not leave the congregation, the church would get a restraining order against them. Further, they were warned that if they repeated any of this to others, the church would bring a lawsuit against them.

In all of this, in spite of all the evidence to the contrary, Pastor Carlton's wife and the church leaders sided with Pastor Carlton and his story. He painted Deanna as a seducer and himself as the loving pastor, nobly resisting her advances, while trying to help her and her husband with their marriage.

Deanna and her husband were broken and disillusioned. They felt terribly betrayed by someone whom they not only had trusted, but also had loved. Both of them had come from unhealthy backgrounds, and neither had gone to any other church before this one. In their search for God and in their openness to faith, this church had become their extended family.

It took them a few months before they stabilized enough to say to themselves and to each other, "This is not about God. This is about some really messed up people." They then decided they would try another place of worship. Their first effort, however, was met with further disappointment. Pastor Carlton's wife had discovered where the couple was attending services and had called the pastor there to issue a warning about them. Not having felt welcome in this new church, the couple moved on, only later to learn of the phone call.

After a few more months at home, their faith in themselves and in God prodded them to try yet another church. This new pastor was different. He visited the couple together in their home. He sensed a resistance to his getting too close, and so he asked them about their fears in becoming active in the church. After some gentle poking and prodding, Deanna and her husband opened up to him about the misconduct of Pastor Carlton and the way they had been treated. This new pastor immediately called what they had experienced abuse. He went on to talk about a sacred trust a pastor has, and he apologized, as a minster, to both of them. They were shocked. They had never heard this before.

The betrayal and disappointment they had felt, now gave way to a flood of anger. "How could Pastor Carlton lie to us?" they both asked.

"How could I have believed this sickness?" Deanna wanted to know. She felt labeled: "I am the woman the pastor touched. I'm the one he violated," she said. "I just want to vomit."

Deanna went back into therapy. This time, it was with a fully credentialed, licensed therapist. The therapist apologized, as a man, for what had been done to her. He helped her piece her life back together. She learned about abuse and discovered she had options, that she did not have to remain a victim.

Deanna also learned about the "forbidden zone" between pastor and parishioner, counselor and client, doctor and patient, boss and employee, mentor and mentee, etc. These relationships have areas that are termed "forbidden" because of the unequal balance of power, because of the tremendous potential for violation in place of helping. Power that heals is manna. Power that destroys is taboo. When that taboo is broken, then the sacred trust to act in the vulnerable person's best interest is also broken. Deanna learned that, in such a relationship, when someone crosses that line, it produces in the victim profound damage, including confusion, suicidal fantasies, emotional instability, sexual dysfunction, guilt, shame, inability to trust. What she was feeling in her relationship with Pastor Carlton was normal. She was not crazy, as she had been told she was.

The unbelievable irony is that, in all of the aftermath of the situation with Rev. Abuser (as Deanna had begun calling him), he shamelessly continued to call her and her husband as if nothing had happened or as if, regardless of what happened or what others said or did, *his* feelings toward them remained unchanged and he still considered them his dear friends and wanted to continue to try to help them with their problem.

But Deanna was getting stronger. Not only was she resisting Rev. Abuser's continued advances, she also decided to sue. She filed a complaint with the police, pressed charges for criminal sexual conduct, got herself an attorney, and started a lawsuit against Pastor Carlton and the church.

They counterfiled a lawsuit against her. She endured being laughed at, being labeled as sick and crazy, and being subjected to testing by a psychiatrist. The church called in all its contacts and friends in influential positions to prevent having the story published. This high-profile church and its leaders were able to divert attention onto Deanna, portraying her as a "Jezebel" who was attempting to bring down a respected member of the community.

What no one bothered to explore (or else chose not to wait around to find out) was the way it ended. Deanna was awarded a large sum of money by the mediation panel that reviewed the case. Mysteriously, no newspaper bothered with the story.

Rev. Abuser is still preaching. However, Deanna's new pastor confronted him about the abuse. The man's church had already decided to ignore Pastor Carlton's behavior. Deanna's new pastor threatened public exposure if Carlton continued preaching outside his own church as he had frequently done. Pastor Carlton still tries occasionally, but Deanna, her pastor, and the elders of the church she now attends keep heading him off at the pass. They decided that if they couldn't appeal to his conscience, they'd appeal to his pocketbook.

Profile

Pastor Carlton was the youngest of a number of children born to missionary parents. The poverty he endured growing up was only slightly offset by the honor bestowed on his family because of their work in the ministry.

As he grew up, he realized his gift of oratory. People listened to him, and he was attractive. He decided to stay in an urban church. In that setting, he had a vast pool from which to draw people into his congregation.

His unusual presentation became a magnet for his church, which grew rapidly. His reputation also grew, and his congregation was not only proud of him, but also proud to be part of his church. His somewhat unsophisticated flock felt empowered by having their pastor live well, drive a luxury car, and run with the important people of their city.

He was given such free reign that even when he used shocking or profane language from his pulpit, he was excused as "just trying to get their attention" by using things of the world. Pastor Carlton took what he thought (which was what he taught his congregation to believe) to be the "high road." Like sheep, the people followed, believing and obeying.

Over the years, a number of abusive situations occurred within Pastor Carlton's congregation. There were women who were stalked, women who were physically abused, and attempted rapes. His approach to dealing with these situations was to give a symbolic slap on the wrist to the perpetrator. Then he would admonish the female victims to forgive and forget and warned them to be sure that they had not invited or did not deserve what had happened to them. He then would firmly state, "We are here for everyone, even those with problems."

When restraining orders were issued by a judge against any of the men in his church, he refused to honor them, citing separation of church and state. He even wrote letters to the judge on behalf of these men. His attitude was that since they were part of his congregation, they must be deserving men. He chastised the women for resorting to that sort of thing, and from his pulpit, he emphatically said, "It is wrong for a Christian ever to get a restraining order!" He would quote scripture out of context to bolster his position. He told his congregation that all issues concerning people in his church should be settled in his church and not in the courts. When any of the women expressed fear for themselves or for other women in the church, he told them they were vengeful liars, troublemakers, sinful adolescents, and that they were gossips. Eventually, those women left his church; the men are still there.

Clearly Pastor Carlton was vicariously enjoying the dominant treatment of men over women, as he himself was practicing. He thrived on his power over his subjects and relished his position as a man among men. He enjoyed his identification with the aggressor in the abusive men in his congregation.

Mrs. Carlton exhibited a similar desire for dominance in her being married to a powerful, successful man. She was willing to live in gross denial of his philandering rather than leave her position as his wife. She felt powerful in being aligned with him.

(In the same way, Deanna's mother had remained in denial. Her raging, abusive husband was easier to handle if she closed her eyes to what he was doing and just went along with things. Sadly, she sacrificed not just her own integrity but also her own children on the altar of personal comfort and convenience.)

In the final analysis, Pastor Carlton was comfortable only with women who would look up to him and who never would challenge him. In his inner circle, there was no room for difference of opinion, especially from a woman.

As Part of her recovery process, Deanna wrote these poems.

SHAME ON YOU

Shame on you
they all said
for trusting a man of the cloth
ordained
by heaven and earth
to help the hurting and wounded

Shame on you
for believing his flattery
smoother than oil
that convinced you
to do the unthinkable
you really didn't expect him
to tell the truth,
did you?

about how he touched you,
took advantage of you
exploited your
little girl inside
who came out because he said
it was safe
and how he ripped off your life
your innocence and your "you"
until there was nothing left but
raw nerve, hate, madness, fear

Shame on you
sinister minister
for touching little girls
in big bodies
who only need a hug.

THE 'LAZY BOY'

He was too lazy to consider my feelings
how touching me here and there
would not ease my pain
but bring more
when it was discovered
what he's done.

He was too lazy
to tell the truth
about how he said
it was OK, this is the way
people who love each other act
out their fantasies
or nightmares.

He was too lazy to find out
love doesn't
pull down your stockings
and pull up your dresses
and do stuff that you
really shouldn't do
that love doesn't look out for itself
while ignoring everybody else,
especially me.

He was too lazy to say
I was wrong
I shouldn't have
wounded you
hurt you
lied to you,
that afternoon
on the blue plaid La-Z-Boy couch.

INSIGHTS

A Charmer is adept at normalizing his behavior. For the victim who is entangled with him, the experience is much like that of the adult child of an alcoholic; the victim isn't able to know what normal is.

A Charmer actually believes his behavior is invisible. Like the emperor with no clothes, he thinks the world doesn't see what he's doing. Either that, or he doesn't see anything questionable about what he's doing.

The "specialness" that a Charmer feels about himself is real to him. Therefore, he needs to be surrounded by "special" people who can also see his "specialness."

Though the Charmer considers truth an intrusion in his agenda, he is very good at exhibiting great concern for it. The reality is, however, that he views his own thoughts and words as ultimate truth.

Singles Groups

One of the great recent contributions to the community (though it is also one of the new potential dangers the church faces) is in the explosion of singles ministries. Because of the skyrocketing divorce rate over the past twenty-five years, churches have begun to focus on a growing mission field in their own backyard. In an effort to provide support and encouragement for people whose lives have been shattered by divorce, programs for recovery from this trauma have been developed, along with opportunities for constructing a new social life with other singles. The healing possibilities and the restoration of self-esteem and confidence are nothing short of miraculous (see my book *Starting Again: A Divorce Recovery Program*).

Traditionally, people who've attended church have done so because they've had a reasonable expectation of what they are likely to hear. With that in mind, they've listened to what is taught. Then at some point, they've made a decision as to whether or not they will buy in to the good news of salvation for themselves, as well as to whether or not they will come back to the church.

In a singles group, however, many are drawn for the sole purpose of having a place to be, of having an opportunity to socialize with others like themselves, and of having the chance to reconnect with someone for dating and mating. Through this "back door" of social need, many singles have found more than they sought; they have found a new faith and a place in the church itself.

Due to the great need and hunger for this kind of ministry, churches who have been attentive to singles issues have grown very quickly through outreach in this sphere. In fact, in a relatively short time, some churches have found their singles to make up almost half of their entire church population. Ministry to singles has proven to be the most effective means of bringing people into the church in the last twenty years.

The downside to this scenario is that this kind of ministry draws many people who are not necessarily interested in spiritual issues. There are often personal agendas in the group that include the same attitudes and behaviors that were part of life in singles bars and other secular activities. They are the ones who are probably divorced for very good reasons. For a number of them, their agendas are not subject to change. Their purpose is fixed, and they are impervious to any accompanying message they might hear.

However, as long as there are standards and boundaries, singles ministries can still remain an acceptable technique for bringing people under the influence of the church and spirituality– people who might never come any other way.

The dangers are in the covert activities of some group members. The larger the group, the more difficult it is to know what is truly going on. It requires increased structure and awareness. Here is where the Charmer and con artist shine. Those who are overt—obvious in their desires and intentions—are often confronted at the point of violation and stopped in one way or another. But the Charmer has the ability to move easily within the group without detection and, if necessary, to lose himself in the crowd. If group leaders have not developed specific awareness in spotting and dealing with a Charmer, even *they* can be taken in as easily as anyone. When this happens, the Charmer has an open field.

And what an opportunity for deception! For a woman, it is especially precarious. She goes to a church singles meeting, wounded from a broken relationship, vulnerable and frightened. If she meets a kind, sensitive man there, she is particularly trusting because of having met him in church. In her neediness, she overlooks the fact that meeting him at church does not automatically make him a godly man, or even a moral man. (After all, being born in a bakery does not make one a doughnut!)

Without knowing it or intending to do so, a church can facilitate the abuse of unsuspecting people. Churches need to educate their staff and lay workers (particularly in a singles or children's ministry) to identify and deal with those who would use or abuse others within their organization. Church leaders need to own the responsibility for preventing the kind of ignorance and silence that would appear to the Charmer as a sanctioning of his violation and victimizing others in the church.

It is important that a church take steps to be sure it is not allowing a wolf in sheep's clothing in among wounded, trusting sheep. A pastor is to shepherd the flock, which includes protecting it. It is inexcusable and unforgivable for clergy to reject facts or refuse to be educated on issues of any kind of abuse.

Probably in no other activity of the church (with the possible exception of children's programs) will a leader be challenged with as much potential confrontation and problem-solving as in a singles ministry.

There are many people in churches who have a bad experience and simply don't return. Then there are those who have a damaging encounter, report it to no avail, and subsequently leave because of double disappointment. For these people, they must process not only the aftermath of the abuse, but also their disillusion with the very church they had trusted to give understanding and support. For them, their entire encounter with the church has been negative, and they feel betrayed.

This is not meant to call for or to justify a "witch hunt." However, when incidents are reported or do occur, if an organization does not provide proper attention to and resolution of these matters, that organization is acting irresponsibly, and its neglect is injurious to victims. People have the right to feel safe, especially at church. It is not just another public place. The church must be careful not to be a sanctuary for perpetrators at the expense of innocent people.

A singles group can provide enormous opportunities for people with ill motives. If issues are not properly addressed, the group will end up losing many good people who get scared away by the not-so-good people who end up staying. Eventually, this negative pattern will change the whole complexion of the group. The group's quality and attractiveness to newcomers diminishes, and the reputation of the whole church can be damaged.

One of the better ideas for carrying on this kind of ministry has been implemented in the Catholic Alumni Club. Though rules vary from state to state, some group activities are open to non-Catholics, as long as the individual is part of the Christian faith and espouses Christian values. To join, one must produce proof of one's marital status, provide character information, and pay a membership fee.

The group is designed for socializing and cooperative efforts for charitable and other worthwhile events. Anyone who falls short of the group's marital status and behavior requirements is not permitted to participate. The rules are stated, and one must agree to them or else be denied membership. If a member is discovered in violation of the standards, he or she is eliminated from the club.

Reasonable guidelines are set to provide as much safety and security as possible. The expectations placed on members and on their behavior are established from the beginning. These parameters are the standard against which all may be measured should anything become a problem. Such rules also serve to provide better coverage for the church's liability.

When considering this kind of ministry to singles, a divorce-recovery program could be open-ended. However, the ongoing social-club part of a singles ministry should have definite parameters, especially when a group grows beyond twenty to twenty-five in number.

Action Needed: Therapy and Accountability

Any perpetrator needs to be removed from the group for the protection of others. (Even secular organizations have boundaries for the sake of their membership if one member is found to be abusing another.)

If a group member who is behaving inappropriately is serious about changing and getting help for his problem, he should be willing to go into therapy and be held accountable for his behaviors, both public and private. His compliance, or lack thereof, will verify his sincerity in getting help for his problem.

It is extremely difficult for a Charmer really to see what his problem is or what it does to others. It is also very unlikely that he will submit himself to accountability, which is a good indication of his intentions in the first place.

Tony

He was drop-dead gorgeous: black patent-leather colored eyes on a manly, chiseled face with thick, dark, slightly wavy hair, and deep dimples à la Tom Selleck. His tall, slender build was that of a matinèe idol in his late forties. His countenance alternated between the playful, impish look of an elf and that of a brooding poet. He appeared quiet and shy until he could establish a one-on-one relationship, and then he focused so intently on the person he was with, that the person would become enraptured and captive. A woman would be torn between her desire to mother him and her impulse to go to bed with him. The latter usually won out.

Tony was a toucher. He had a technique for drawing women to himself in a seemingly nurturing, compassionate way. His hug held a promise of secret communion, and to others it had the definite look of two people who were lovers. He was impulsive in a way that made for spontaneous fun, a serendipitous adventure for anyone around him. He could probe ever so subtly to glean very personal revelations from others (which he would later use against them, if needed). But he was very secretive and noncommittal about his own life.

Tony had become interested in Susan, a woman at the singles group they both attended. She was attractive and vivacious, so they made a handsome couple. But it was an unusual combination—one that was difficult for most of their friends to understand. She was what many would call a "goody two shoes." He was a swinger with the reputation of being a serious womanizer. They were like Sky Masterson and Sarah Brown right out of *Guys and Dolls*.

Tony was patient, standing back and sizing up situations before he jumped in. He watched Susan for eight months, occasionally saying hello or making some comment to start a conversation with her. She responded in a friendly way, as she did with just about everyone, but not in the way most women responded to Tony. In his conversations with other women, after his first few words, the woman would usually become the aggressor. He almost never asked anyone for a date. He didn't have to. He was bombarded constantly with invitations and offers from females.

But Susan was an old-fashioned woman, and she wasn't in the habit of calling men, especially men she didn't know. So after Tony realized that the hints he'd been dropping weren't producing the usual results, he began calling Susan periodically with brief, idle conversation. Still, she did not pursue him. Finally he called and asked her for a date.

Besides finding Tony quite appealing, Susan was also very trusting, especially since she had met him at church, so she accepted his invitation.

Susan was fun to be with, a self-confident woman who was open and warm. When she complimented Tony during their first evening out together, mentioning how attractive she found him, he acted put off and said, "I resent that. I don't want just to be liked for what people think of my looks."

Refreshing, she thought. That had been one of her struggles too. Just because she was attractive, she didn't want to be thought of as just another pretty face. They had found a point of connection. Immediately, they enjoyed each others' company, and there was definitely chemistry between them.

They dated for a year—a rather stormy year. Whenever they had a disagreement, it was because Tony had never dealt with a healthy, assertive woman. She didn't like being told she was controlling just because she disagreed with Tony, had her own opinion, or expected him to honor his word. She insisted that Tony treat her with respect and that he honor her standards. As for Tony, he was used to being in control of his relationships. He was not used to being with a woman who wanted a mutual and reciprocal relationship, who expected to receive as well as give. Whenever he felt himself participating in that unfamiliar arrangement, he felt threatened and vulnerable, so he would create distance, sabotaging the closeness. But he always came back when he saw that his way of handling the situation didn't produce the desired result in Susan.

As time went on, Tony became more invested in the future of their relationship than Susan was. For Tony, Susan represented a challenge and a fear that he might be losing his touch.

Time after time, Susan complained of receiving mixed messages from Tony and of never knowing what she could trust about him. Time after time, she would throw up her hands and walk away in exhausted frustration. But each time she did, Tony would come after her. He refused to take no for an answer. He would apologize, cajole, or just keep hanging around, popping in and out of her life until he could catch her at a time when she no longer felt angry with him. Then he would charm his way back into her good graces. Most of the time, he would just act as if nothing had happened, do his best to make her laugh, and send her a romantic card or gift. Tony was wildly romantic. He had all the right moves women dream of, except in the practical areas.

When Tony was behaving himself, Susan enjoyed being with him. He *was* fun, so she'd find herself giving in again. But resentment kept building inside of her because they never really resolved their differences; Tony just managed to suppress or evade them. All the while, Susan thought she was standing her ground with Tony. She had no idea that he was carrying out his own plan where and when no one was watching.

After the year of chaotic dating, of beautiful highs and ugly lows, Susan decided she'd had enough and ended their relationship. Tony had begun to talk about marriage. Susan was not looking for a husband. If she decided to remarry, she wanted more stability in a relationship, more integrity, and a lot less pain than she saw possible with Tony. There were too many differences in their value systems to share a lifetime together. And for Susan, there was an unsettling inner feeling that his real need was to control her and the relationship.

For a while, Tony had been able to make just enough concessions, just often enough to effectively distract Susan from catching on to him. But after a year of dating, Susan had no confidence in Tony's love for her. He just wanted her to be in his control.

No woman, other than his ex-wife, had ever ended a relationship with Tony. But now Susan was turning him away, insisting that their relationship was over. He resented her statement that because of their religious differences, she would never consider marrying him.

For the next six months, Tony casually dated one woman after another in his old manner, but he still called frequently to see if Susan was dating anyone else. When he called, he'd make sure she knew he was not sitting home alone.

At one point, Tony told Susan he thought she should also date. Her response was, "I will date if and when I choose to, and I don't need your permission. I'm not going to go out just to make you feel less guilty about your dating. I know you are dating, and it's fine with me. I never thought you wouldn't." This wasn't the response Tony wanted or expected, and he didn't really know how to handle it. But since Susan wasn't seeing anyone else, he wouldn't be concerned.

Then things changed. Tony heard Susan had started dating some-one, and he went crazy. He wanted to know all about it. He probed for answers. No matter how Susan gently tried to say that it was really none of his business, Tony was invasive and impolite in his search for information. He would take any opportunity to question what it was Susan saw in this man, to find fault in him, and then to try making her feel guilty with statements, such as, "You're only interested in him because he has a big job and a better car than mine."

After a night out with her new friend, Susan heard from Tony, who let her know that he was well aware of the date, of where they had gone, and of how late the man had stayed at Susan's house. She was furious at this invasion of her privacy and was even more determined to stay away from Tony.

Tony, however, would "just happen" to show up many places she went: the airport, theaters, grocery stores, shopping malls. He left candy and flowers under the wiper blades of her car, in her mailbox, or at her front door. He seemed always to know where she was. He was obsessed with her. He told her that he couldn't sleep, that he went through several prescriptions of Valium, that he suffered horrible headaches, and that he became physically ill when he went more than a few days without seeing her.

He would accuse her of all his own sins: of unfaithfulness, lying, cheating. He would try to invade her privacy by asking very personal questions. He accused her of keeping secrets and of having something to hide. If she refused to answer his questions or denied his charges, he assumed her guilty of his imaginings and proceeded verbally to beat her up, acting as if his assumptions were fact.

It was a favorite tactic of Tony's to take the focus off his own behavior by changing the subject or distracting attention to someone else in some way.

After two months of carefully monitoring Susan's dating, Tony could no longer contain his anxiety. Intimidation had not worked on Susan, so he tried a new level of persuasion. He pulled her aside and said, "Susan, I love you! Everyone has known it but me. I've never said that to anyone since my divorce ten years ago. Please give us another chance."

Tony seemed so contrite and sincere; he even cried. Susan had once felt lovingly toward him. However, she remembered the reasons she had previously ended the relationship, and she had no intention of getting back into the same old thing. She said she would see him, but not exclusively. If he would accept that, she'd give him another chance to prove himself. He said he would.

Susan also had been honest with the other man she was seeing. From her perspective, they were merely two friends who enjoyed doing things together, and even though he hoped for more than a friendship, he accepted where Susan was in her decision. For a few months, she discretely dated both men. Tony continued the same up-and-down, close-and-distant pattern as before. Susan understood his frustration with her dating someone else, but she wasn't going to date Tony exclusively, as before, unless he showed her something different in his attitude and behavior. So far, it was more of the same, only with more of the lows.

Then Tony told Susan he had experienced a dramatic religious conversation. He described it in great detail. "I've been a whore all my life," Tony told her, "and I don't want that anymore. You're everything I ever wanted in a woman. You've shown me a side of life I never knew existed, and I want that kind of life. Just you and me and our children, that's all I want." He said he knew his behavior had been wrong, but he wanted to change all that.

Susan assumed he was truly a changed man. This was a big breakthrough; the biggest obstacle in their way was now gone. She began really considering a serious relationship with him now. She even stopped seeing the other man to concentrate on Tony. But once Susan stopped dating anyone else, Tony reverted back to the same old behaviors and attitudes. Once again, Susan was taken in.

He had talked about marriage from early in their relationship. Now that Susan believed that he was really trying to change and now that she had stopped seeing anyone else, Susan wanted to meet his children. In the two years since they met, she had included him in her family activities during the times they were dating, but he always made excuses or just ignored her inquiries about telling his family about their relationship. When she pressed him for an answer, he had none. Susan felt manipulated, but Tony always had the correct responses to all her doubts.

Again Susan ended their relationship. Things went back to the way they were before, and Tony persisted in trying to win her back again. He insisted that the reason he did such desperate things was because he was so lovesick and insecure in their relationship. He kept assuring her he would be very different if only he could count on a future with her. But this time she was determined not to let him back into her life.

Several months went by, and a number of Susan's friends suggested she give the relationship with Tony one more try, this time giving him the assurances he needed and seeing if that would make a difference. Susan finally agreed again to an exclusive relationship and to explore the possibility of a future together, provided she and Tony told his children the nature of their relationship and that the two of them went to joint counseling to see if they really could transcend their differences. Tony dragged his feet for several weeks on the counseling issue, but finally he reluctantly agreed.

For a while things were euphoric. Tony and Susan were caught up in that wonderful oceanic feeling that only two people in love can understand. The counseling sessions were difficult, but the two of them persevered. They began making plans for the future, looking at rings and houses.

Tony, however, just wouldn't get beyond his jealousy, his possessiveness, and his lack of trust. Susan had never had anyone question her integrity before, but Tony suspiciously questioned her about almost everything. In addition, Tony still would neither tell his children about the relationship nor have them around Susan.

One day Tony admitted to Susan that he had found a way into her home when she was not there, had rummaged through her things to find her private journal, and had read it from start to finish, not just once, but on two different occasions. He said he needed to know everything she was thinking, how she felt, and the struggles she had. Susan felt violated, betrayed, emotionally raped. Of course, he had brought his own interpretation to what he'd read, and he felt justified in satisfying his curiosity.

That should have ended the courtship for good. However, Susan was so stunned and numbed with disbelief of what he had done, not yet realizing its full significance, that she even tried to get beyond it and continue the counseling. But her growing anger at his invasion was more than she could forgive this time. Tony argued, blamed, and fought to hang on. He refused to accept responsibility for having done something wrong. He knew he had blown his last chance with Susan.

Then, everything changed dramatically. Susan received a phone call from Tony's ex-wife, Connie, whose opening statement was this: "Will you please keep Tony away from me! I just found out he's been seeing you all this year, as well as seeing me. He's treated me like his whore for twenty-five years. He always counted on my shyness to keep me from confronting any of his women. Well, I've had enough!"

Connie's stories of her relationship with Tony (during their marriage and even after their divorce) revealed a dance of pain in which they continued punishing each other with their personal weapons. His arsenal consisted of flaunting his affairs and relationships, along with the freedoms and activities he enjoyed—all the things that characterized the bachelor life he had always maintained. Hers included withholding approval, affection, and communication; she would withdraw from him except to criticize or treat him with disdain. They would, however, rush at each other in a sexual frenzy, even though they might not speak to each other for weeks at a time before or after such encounters.

Susan was stunned. As the two women continued to talk, comparing stories, it became evident that Tony had never stopped his sexual involvement with Connie, even after years of being divorced! Needless to say, Connie's problems were as big as Tony's, though less lethal. The two of them were enmeshed and entangled in each other's lives in a mutually addictive pattern and would not break free. In fact, Connie was the first person to whom Tony would go when he and Susan were not seeing each other. In his own mind, Tony had felt justified in doing so, since Susan was not cooperating with his agenda and refused to have a sexual relationship with him. In truth, even if Susan had, Tony would have continued his relationship with Connie. For him, one woman would never be enough. Monogamy would diminish his image of himself as a real man. During the entire time he and Susan had been dating, Tony had been able to lead a double life. He had, in fact, become a master of it to everyone.

Susan later recalled a number of things Tony had said to her in their conversations, things she had naively dismissed as part of his humor. If she questioned any of his statements, he always said he was joking. Now she was realizing that he had been serious, that he'd been testing her limits of tolerance and naiveté. His inappropriate use of humor had been a frequent irritant and point of conflict between them.

On a few occasions, Tony had taken Susan to events with one of his children. She now realized that Tony's daughter had to witness their father's flaunting his unsuspecting girlfriend, even while she and her brothers knew he was bedding their mother at the same time. It seemed the only one who knew nothing of what was going on was Susan. Tony denied nothing but rationalized that Susan had driven him to it by doing this or that or by not doing something else.

Susan could only apologize to Connie and her children. She had been an unknowing pawn in Tony's chess game. She felt as if she had been dating a married man, an idea of such repugnance to her that it made her physically ill. While she felt sorry for Connie and her children, she herself felt used, abused, and cheated out of more than two years of her life. It would take a long time for her to work through her shock, anger, and grief.

This had finally done it for Susan. She woke up. There was now a reality that could never again be denied, rationalized, or excused. She had been naive, a slow learner, but once she got it, a corner was turned. She was angry at herself for being too trusting, for believing a leopard could change its spots, for thinking that no one is beyond changing. And although she still believes (because of her faith in God's transforming power) that people can change, she also has come to realize that some people don't want or intend to change. Such individuals will try to get around real change any way possible, hoping still to reap good rewards while remaining the same and always in control of their own lives. As Dr. M. Scott Peck says, "Even God cannot heal a person who does not want to be healed"[10]

The irony of this story is that later when Susan had to bring charges against Tony for stalking and harassing her, over the following year, Connie would testify in court to defend her ex-husband. Connie was typical of the abused woman syndrome.

Tony still continues his double life, taking advantage of unsuspecting women. Meanwhile, Connie hates herself for having such a lack of self-respect that she continues to give in to Tony. Her self-esteem suffers again and again as she sinks lower into the quicksand of her addiction to him. It's been several more years now since Tony's relationship with Susan ended, but Connie and Tony will probably be in the same cycle for many years to come.

Profile

Tony was the beautiful, quiet child of a large Italian family on Chicago's South Side. His father had been abusive in every way to the mother and children. Pornography was commonplace in their household. The father had openly had other women, relationships about which he boasted loudly in front of his children. The father murdered one of his mistresses and was acquitted of the crime. He finally deserted the family for good, leaving them destitute.

Combined feelings of anger, abandonment, and betrayal washed over the family and stayed there. The debris of messages left with them included the following:

- Women have no rights, only responsibilities to a man.
- Men have the right to do whatever, whenever they please.
- If it feels good, do it.
- It isn't wrong if you can get away with it.
- A conscience is a weakness.
- Don't really trust anyone; they'll get you if you don't get them first.

As a result, the family members trusted no one—not even each other. Most of the time, they didn't even speak to each other. At other times, they were fiercely loyal to the point of being ridiculous.

When the children had to be farmed out to other families for survival, somehow Tony maneuvered to be the only one left with his mother. He learned early on what to say and do to please, and he understood when to stay out of the way or be silent. In the years to come, when he saw what all the abuse and splintering of the family had done to his siblings, he would have a deep sense of survival guilt. As penance, he became the self-appointed caretaker for all the family's problems. This assumed role would often be misunderstood and resented.

Tony had often said to Susan that he wanted to take care of her, which explained why he was out-of-control when she exhibited independence. He had loved Connie, he said, because she was timid and shy. However, when Connie finally confronted him about his bad behavior in the marriage, she removed herself from his caretaking. When she divorced him because of his womanizing, it was the ultimate rejection of his caretaking and manipulation. He would continue to punish her for that by refusing to stay away, playing on her love and her addiction to him, which allowed him to use her sexually at his whim. Sometimes Tony would tell Connie that he still loved only her, but if Connie objected to Tony's continuing his other relationships, Tony would remind her, "We're not married anymore. I can see anyone I please."

When Connie had divorced Tony, she had played right into his hands. If she weakened about remarrying him, however, Tony would distance himself again. He enjoyed the challenge and romance of the chase, but he lost interest when the goal was reached. He was angry she'd divorced him, but he didn't want to remarry her. Why should he? Now he had the best of both worlds and without needing to sneak around or having anyone trying to make him accountable for his behavior. Connie was Tony's "ace in the hole," someone to use for safe sex. He would use her to make sure he could still have her if he wanted her, and then he'd leave again.

Connie and Susan were the only women who'd ever made any demands on Tony. He would meet their demands only to get what he wanted in the way of a commitment from them, to know he could have them. Then he'd back off to recreate the crisis and the chase again. With Connie, he got the sex he wanted. With Susan, he was after a lifestyle he'd never known existed and opportunities to experience life on the other side of the tracks.

Tony believed he really loved and wanted Susan, but he wouldn't let go of the security of his secret, backup life. He couldn't see, as Susan finally came to realize, that she was a giant conquest that he could use to make himself feel secure, in control of his world, and less vulnerable to chance. He truly did not see anything wrong in his doing this; although he would not want anyone to treat him the way he treated women.

The family in which Tony grew up would establish a pattern of violence and abuse, including murder, especially toward women. They were "macho men." The measure of their prowess, of their manhood, depended on how many women they could get and have, as well as what they could get those women to put up with or do for them. Tony's father and brothers lacked the social skills to convince and persuade, so they demanded and took. They have violent tempers and continue their abusive ways.

As children, Tony and his siblings were psychologically abused by the perpetuated messages of distortion of male and female roles and by the definition of relationships. One brother mimicked his father's crime but was not so fortunate as his father in having the consequences dismissed. He's in prison for life for his rapes and murders. Two of the remaining brothers won't allow Tony in their homes. One of them says he doesn't like the way Tony acts around his wife.

Once he lost Susan, Tony gave up on trying to rise above his background. It was easier for him to go the other way. Susan was a hard act to follow; he never again found anyone like her. He's back to dating a succession of women with whom he never maintains a relationship for more than two or three months.

Tony deluded himself in thinking he had not become part of the abuse from his past. He believed he was different, that he was caring. But Tony had become like his family. He abuses with charm. His victims just don't know what hit them nor that they suffer the kind of injury that is perhaps best symbolized by someone who is bleeding internally.

INSIGHTS

When a man tells a woman he isn't good enough for her, she should listen and run. He knows something she doesn't.

The flip side of the Charmer is the abuser—someone who can't make things work for himself anymore or someone who never could make things work any other way. Sexual addiction is often a disguise for a desire for violence or hatred toward women: "killing them softly with his love."

The Charmer will often do a series of kindnesses as a smoke screen or as a nonverbal barter for your silence or lack of confrontation of his behaviors or attitudes. His use of flowers, cards, or other seemingly loving gestures is generally a means of diverting attention away from anything that would make him accountable.

It was a pivotal point in time when Tony was finally confronted and held accountable for the inappropriateness of his behavior. At that juncture, an important choice was made. With his conscience fully alerted, he rejected the opportunity to turn away from continuing in the wrong direction. At that point, Tony ceased to be a Charmer and crossed the line to con artist.

The con artist knows full well what he is doing and chooses to do the wrong thing, to make the evil, destructive choice. He doesn't mind that he hurts others, as long as he's getting what he wants.

The Charmer is a master manipulator who can quickly zero in on one's points of weakness and vulnerability and attack there. An individual with a more crude, less developed charm will pick the most vulnerable or trusting victim he can find and act quickly before she catches on. Those with the lowest skill level in utilizing charm and communication are the ones who most quickly become abusive.

In the case study of Tony, his stalking and harassment were proven in court. He ignored a warrant for his arrest, had to be tracked down by police, and was placed under a restraining order by the court. He confessed to everything he'd done to both Susan and Connie, but continued monitoring Susan's life and harassing her, as did his friends and members of his family. Investigation revealed he had been under a restraining order other times. He was allowed to continue participating as he had previously in the singles group at the church. Without consequences for his behavior, he most likely will repeat it with other women. The church's position was naively stated as "We are here for everyone – even those with problems."

As an outsider, Connie's view continues to be that the church condones Tony's behavior and that the singles group is "just another meat market."

Not surprisingly, Susan never again felt safe or comfortable in that singles group. She left. It took months for her to work through the posttraumatic stress she suffered. And feeling abandoned and betrayed by her church, and it's leaders, Susan never again felt the same about attending there.

PROFESSIONAL CHARMERS:
EXAMPLES FROM
THE BUSINESS WORLD

A LL IS FAIR in love and war," or so the saying goes. But is it true?

Love and war: For many people, making a living falls into one or both of these categories, particularly if there is much to be gained. The stories are commonplace enough: the doctor, attorney, politician, or entrepreneur who leaves the forty-year-old wife who put him through graduate school; the businessman who divorces the woman who reared his children, entertained his clients, and supported him on his way up; or the disadvantaged kid who, with his childhood sweetheart by his side, fights his way to the top of the heap and then abandons her for someone flashier. All are examples of Charmers who (because of the publicity they've received, the press clippings, or their idealized view of themselves) now believe that they deserve a trophy wife or perhaps a mistress or at least to get rid of any evidence that their success was not won all by themselves.

With their bigger audience, these Charmers have less and less time to spend on mundane things, such as being involved much with family, or on activities that don't yield maximum notoriety for the time spent. Such Charmers have arrived in the eyes of their audiences. If surrounding themselves with all the accouterments of success will perpetuate the grandiose image they have of themselves (and which others also have of them), then it becomes easy for them to rationalize any decisions that need to be made.

It's not easy to resist the "groupies" who hang around, flatter, and offer themselves just to be part of the Charmer's entourage. What a heady experience! *I must be better than even I imagined or dreamed possible!* the Charmer begins to think. It takes the "right stuff" to resist that kind of enticement. And in truth, we never really know what we're made of until we are tested. Just like new drugs, mathematics, science—theories that become fact when applied to life, so it is with personal integrity—it must survive testing.

And contrary to the rationalization that "Everybody does it," there are legions of people who don't. When we seek to rationalize our own behavior, we tend to take our polls from the group that will best justify whatever we're trying to prove. The ones who shout out this kind of rationale have taken their lead from the ones who do what they themselves want to do, not from objective pollsters. Not very scientific, but then, character can't be measured in a test tube.

There are many in business, entertainment, and the sports world who are exemplary in their methods of doing business and in their personal lives. They are people who decided ahead of time the kind of person they will be, with or without career success.

We must, at this point, understand that success is not the problem. It is one's attitude about his or her success that can become problematic. It is interesting to note that for every person of great wealth or accomplishment who handles success well, there are hundreds of people who handle better still their mediocrity or even their poverty.

Yes, maybe it's because these less-fortunate individuals haven't been tested in their ability to manage fame and fortune. But perhaps the reality is that they are simply more content.

For the Charmer, the lure of fame and fortune are strong. And because there are so many tangible rewards in the business world, it becomes easy for him to ignore the intangible, the intrinsic inner rewards of good character and integrity.

O. J. Simpson

He went from what many called "the greatest football running back of the century" to what many others called "the murderer in the crime of the century."

His early celebrity on the West Coast began in high school, where he broke records in his sport.

Even before his fame as an athlete, he enjoyed living on the edge, flirting with danger, and seeing what petty crimes he could get away with. He started running with a fast crowd, leading a gang, and getting into one scrap after another. He was involved in frequent thefts (he just couldn't stay out of trouble) all before even reaching his teen years. He loved to live dangerously, teetering on the brink of disaster at times. A friend described him as one who courted death.

He was not very successful academically, but he loved the fame and privilege he got from playing football. His high-school coach tried to teach him that there are rules in this world that must be obeyed. O. J. listened but did as he pleased.

It was football and avoiding going to Vietnam that lured him to college, and even that was on a dare. After leading his team at the community college he attended to record-winning victories, he was pursued by scores of colleges and universities with offers for full-ride scholarships. He decided that if he was going to college, he wanted it to be the University of Southern California.

O. J. was a runner. He was extraordinary. Many in his ranks believe he was the best of any. At USC, he broke record after record—many of which still stand—and took the Trojans to the Rose Bowl. For himself, he was voted All American, and he won the Heisman Trophy by the largest margin of votes ever.

As the number-one draft pick upon entering the professional ranks, O. J. ended up going to the Buffalo Bills, much to his disappointment. He would be leaving the arena of his fame, as well as parting from friends, family, and sunshine to play in the wicked winters of the Northeast for a last-place team. Both he and his adoring sports fans waged a campaign to get him traded to a team in California—a team more worthy of his exceptional talent. O. J. preferred the glamour of Los Angeles, and his fans there preferred that he not leave. Their efforts, however, failed.

O. J. was expected to make the difference for his new team, but after three bad years in Buffalo, he was depressed and wanted to quit. Then in O. J.'s fourth year as a professional, a new coach arrived in Buffalo, one who catered to O. J.'s talents. Suddenly he was back on his game. He began to perform again. It was the only thing that could put him into a position to get traded back to California.

Once there, he broke into show business by way of commercials. He was the first African-American to become a product spokesperson. He was so popular (with his football fame and his easygoing style, personality, and good looks) that Advertising Age recognized him with the award for Best Presenter in Advertising. For twenty years, he was the spokesperson for the Hertz Corporation until his image changed with the murder of his former second wife, Nicole, and her friend Ron Goldman.

O. J.'s athletic and financial success allowed him to pamper himself, and he garnered trust and admiration from his public. They were willing to excuse any bad behavior. From there, he launched a movie career. He was popular worldwide and became the darling icon of the Black community. He began to believe in his own invincibility and entitlement to ignore the rules. This time, however, there were bigger, more serious rules by which he was refusing to play.

In 1985, he married his second wife, Nicole Brown. Publicly, they were a charmed couple, but privately, it was a turbulent marriage, marked by spousal abuse, calls to the police, and trips to the hospital for Nicole. The battering of his second wife was apparently new behavior, something he had not done in his first marriage.

Even with the bad publicity about his abusive behavior, O. J. managed to continue his career virtually unscathed. He could make the necessary apology and dismiss his behavior as "just something that happened," leaving the impression that it was not a lifestyle. The public never condemned him. Only women's groups began to protest as they became more and more aware of Simpson's private life with Nicole.

Finally, he went too far. In a rage, he murdered Nicole and her friend. He became a fugitive, driving away in his white Bronco, fleeing arrest in the infamous chase scene. The extent of his ability to charm his audience was demonstrated when people cheered him on and encouraged his getaway down the streets of Los Angeles. What other fugitive from justice has ever had that kind of audience?

His public persona—that idealized false self that he believed in—was able to charm people into blindly rooting for him, in spite of the facts. Simpson's enablers were legion. Through a trial that presented mountains of evidence against him, he was able to sustain his public's denial of what had happened, including the members of the jury, who rather than accept the fall of their hero, chose to acquit him. What the whole world knew to be true, was something with which that jury could not come to grips. They wanted and needed their icon. In addition, O. J. had selected a defense attorney who was as much a Charmer as himself. The two together were too much for an unsophisticated group of twelve to see through.

The only thing that hammered away at the injustice of the case was the refusal of Nicole's and Ron's families to accept the verdict. The civil trial showed, to the satisfaction of all the world, that there had been a gross miscarriage of justice. After that trial, anyone who still believed in O. J. Simpson's innocence was obviously not paying attention. Only Simpson himself could maintain a belief in his innocence. No matter the evidence, his ideal self-image still allowed him to believe he didn't murder those two people. In fact, he could probably pass a lie detector test; he's that lost in his delusion.

When O. J. lost the civil trial, he managed to escape the greater portion of accountability and the consequences of his deeds. As he frantically continued his personal search for the killers, going from golf course to golf course (wherever he was allowed to play), he made a telling statement: "Even if I did kill Nicole, wouldn't that prove how much I loved her?" he would ask.

He still doesn't get it. Love does not abuse. Love protects and nurtures. It appears, however, that he reserves the privileges of love only for himself.

Profile

Orenthal James Simpson was born in a ghetto in San Francisco. His father deserted the family when Simpson was only four years old. O. J. suffered from rickets as a child, a condition for which the family was unable to afford medical treatment. His mother, a devout Christian and a courageous parent, made braces for her son, who had become pigeon-toed and bowlegged. Ironically, O. J. signed up for the school track team. His drive and ability to run were the beginning of his introduction to football. Football became his ticket out of the ghetto and into the limelight.

Even as a child, O. J. was charismatic, a leader, and a natural talent. When his run-ins with the law threatened to jeopardize his chances to stay in sports and in school, a friend contacted the famous baseball player Willie Mays, asking him to talk to O. J. Everyone hoped Simpson would listen to his hero, stay out of trouble, and not waste the opportunities that were his for the taking.

By staying in school and excelling in football, he was catapulted into a different world from the one he had known as a child. With his success in college football, he gained a following, he had money, and he could get the things it would take to show everyone else the person he saw himself to be.

He married his childhood sweetheart, but the move to Buffalo took a toll on Simpson's marriage. When he left her behind, in his inattention to their marriage, they separated. When she and the children went back home to California, they drifted still farther apart. In 1979, with the end of his football career and the death of their daughter, their third child, they were divorced.

He played a very busy social field. When he met Nicole Brown, she seemed to be the bridge he needed to get him over the end of his football career and on with life. It's difficult to assess the reasons Simpson began abusing her. If he fits the characteristics of a Charmer, it could be that he believed he had married a trophy wife, one he was never sure he was good enough to hold onto. In his twisted thinking, intimidation and abuse would make her afraid to challenge him or to leave him. He had called the shots in his first marriage, doing whatever he pleased, and *he* had made the decision to leave the marriage. He instinctively knew he could not do that with Nicole.

Another telling statement O. J. has made is this: "There's a lot of BS in life, which I've always done." The arrogant manner in which he made the statement was very revealing of his attitude about himself and life.

With O. J.'s father abandoning him during childhood, this created a great hardship for O. J. and the whole Simpson family. As he grew up, O. J. was deprived of the guidance and restraint he so desperately needed from a father. (Far more delinquents come out of broken homes than out of intact families.)

After his success, O. J. had established a relationship with his estranged dad. By then, however, the damage had been done. And it would eventually become clear that those early issues had never been worked through. In the true fashion of a Charmer, O. J. didn't deal with the past. He just denied its impact, and sought to write on a clean slate.

INSIGHTS

The Charmer believes his own lies and that he is invisible and invincible. Yet he is secretly afraid that he is more vulnerable to being hurt than others are.

Charmers are missing a sense of healthy shame, so they have no problem facing people after hurting someone or after creating a mess.

The Charmer has a strong sense of entitlement, especially if he's "successful." He has a great need to be perceived admirably and will go to great lengths to make sure that happens. He is self-absorbed but very good at camouflaging it.

The Charmer has an underdeveloped conscience, rationalizing right and wrong according to his or her own needs, as immature children do. The more blatant the behaviors of the Charmer, the farther along the continuum he goes in his denial. And the greater the stakes, the more likely he will be to cross the line of pathology, where he no longer knows *or* cares what he does at the expense of others.

Leona Helmsley

She has been described as the Queen of Mean; the epitome of *success* and *excess*; Cinderella corrupted by power and privilege, a fairy tale gone bad. One magazine showed Leona Helmsley's picture with the caption "It Rhymes with Rich." Another showed her with her husband, Harry, on the front cover with three giant green words: "GREED, GREED, GREED."

She fell from grace to become a woman the public loved to hate. It wasn't just that she had fought her way to the top where she had taken on airs of elegance and style above her peers; no, it wasn't, as they say in the South, because "she got above her raisin'." People admire success achieved honestly through hard work and creativity. What people didn't like was her arrogance. Her statement that "Only the little people pay taxes" that destroyed the public's respect and appreciation for her talent and for her accomplishment in creating the lavish home-away-from-home environment in her Helmsley Hotels. Her attitude also did away with any allowances they might make for her.

Leona molded an image of herself, her lifestyle, and her hotels, which became the fantasy she sold to invite people to choose a Helmsley Hotel over other luxury hotels. She believed it was her personal touch that made Helmsley Hotels enticing. She became a visible spokesperson, personally promoting the perfection and details with which guests would be housed and served. She displayed her splendid gowns and donned matching tiaras to do her own advertising, using the slogan "The only palace in the world where the queen stands guard," suggesting that guests would be staying with royalty. She wanted prospective customers to see her rich life and to believe that she wanted to give them everything she herself enjoyed. The hook was clever and very appealing.

Her public image was, however, carefully crafted to hide the reality. One long-term employee stated, "She could woo you to death and turn on you the next minute." That side of her was reserved only for employees or anyone who got in her way. The secret side of Leona was a woman driven by fear of not having enough security, whether in the form of money or love. Admiration meant love to Leona. Money meant power. Power meant security and reasons for others to admire her.

Leona had worked her way up the ladder through two marriages. It was no coincidence that the first husband was a successful attorney and the second husband richer than the first. Both marriages had ended because of her grasping, presumptuous spending of money.

Divorced and with a young son to raise, Leona set about to become rich on her own through real estate. A single mother without even a high-school diploma, she learned to wheel and deal in a world and at a time when not many women—especially uneducated women—had careers. It was neither fashionable nor easy.

Leona met Harry Helmsley just in time to rescue her from herself. She had become a millionaire, but she was on the verge of losing her real-estate license over a questionable deal in which she had intimidated people into purchasing property. A business acquaintance described her as a barracuda. He went on to say she had a sixth sense about what appealed to people, and she would use it shamelessly. She would use whatever it took to make a sale. She used fear and flirted with illegal tactics.

Leona and Harry were meant for each other. Harry pursued Leona until she caught him. She enticed him into a world he had never known. Harry had been a hard-working, nose-to-the-grindstone entrepreneur—a self-made, very wealthy man in real-estate investment. (It was his first wife's money he'd invested to become successful, so marrying for money was something he and Leona had in common.)

Until Harry met Leona, he was happily married to a Quaker wife, living a conservative, simple life.

Leona changed all that. She gave Harry a taste for flair, fun, and extravagance. They made a brilliant team. She had finally met a man with more money than even she could spend. (Over the years, however, she managed to come close.) Together they became New York socialites, giving grand parties and opening new hotels—each one more beautiful than the last.

There were only two things Leona loved more than business: her son, Jay, and her husband, Harry. And she was obsessed with anything she loved. Where Harry was concerned, Leona, now in her fifties, felt as if she had finally met the man of her dreams. She showered him with praise, adoration, and affection. He was considerably older than she. He basked in her flattery and hero worship, and he became utterly captivated. In return, he indulged her completely. In their financial time of trial, he suffered a stroke, and she faced the consequences alone. The other object of Leona's devotion and obsession was her son, who suffered two heart attacks as a young man. He died of a third one at age forty-one. Leona was inconsolable in her grief. That, too, became an obsession. At the same time, she dove farther into her work.

The undoing of the Helmsley empire came, finally, when one of her former employees reported Leona and Harry to the Internal Revenue Service for charging millions of dollars in personal bills to their business expenses as write-offs. Once that story broke, hordes of employees, contractors who had been stiffed, and people Leona had fired and in other ways abused came forward with horror stories about her treatment of them. She was unveiled as a manipulator of people: of employees, financial institutions, the IRS, and the public.

Leona was portrayed in the media as one who set herself up with power and privilege, as one who was impervious to the rules. She was seen as an abusive con artist protecting *her* money, *her* kingdom, *her* image, and *her* reign of terror.

In the end, public opinion cut her down to size. And for breaking the law, she received a tough penalty – prison. Leona went from living in an opulent penthouse, to sharing a small, sparse cell with a stranger.

Profile

Leona was the third daughter of four children born to Jewish immigrants in New York. She remembered her childhood as happy until the Depression. Money problems forced her family to move several times. At one point, the parents were unable to provide for their family of six. They sent Leona to live with relatives for a brief time. She remembers it with deep sadness. She recalls she was the only one sent away.

The family's lack of money had a great impact on Leona's life. It threatened her sense of security within her family unit and then, on a deeper level individually because of her separation from them. She dropped out of high school, but while she had been in school, she had excelled in speech and communication skills. It's not surprising she would use these skills to acquire what she needed to feel safe.

Money was paramount to Leona. She married for it, and her unbridled use of it caused two of her marriages to end in divorce. The third marriage provided unlimited amounts of money, but it was never enough. Individuals who consider themselves deprived of money and the security it represents, often become a bottomless pit. There will never be enough financial resources to fill their perceived need.

Together, Leona and Harry owned 27 hotels, had 30,000 employees, and enjoyed a social life with the elite—a life filled with fun and extravagance. All this, however, was not sufficient for Leona.

She had a need for admiration and to have it all at a minimal cost to herself.

The advertising gimmicks caught the attention of the paying public. Her persona sold Helmsley Hotel rooms and facilities. Her public image and her private image were miles apart. On the other side of her charm was an abusive shrew who would fly into a blind rage at the slightest violation of her perfectionism.

Leona was so self-absorbed, so blind to any pain but her own, that it never occurred to her anyone would expose her. She believed she was in total control of her realm. Even when convicted, Leona was stunned. She really didn't understand why she was being treated this way; after all, in her mind, she had done nothing wrong!

The type of tax-evasion charges against Leona are not that uncommon for people who own their own business; expenses are frequently passed off as client entertainment, business trips, etc. What was uncommon was the punishment meted out to Leona. Compared to the sentences others in similar circumstances had received, Leona's was well overdone.

The public gagged at the thought that Leona and Harry were using personal charm to entice people to spend money at Helmsley Hotels, while laughing and making fun of customers behind closed doors. The public felt insulted and used. People also detested the unfairness of two fabulously wealthy people not paying their fair share of taxes.

During the trial, public opinion carried great weight in deciding Leona's punishment. Harry was incapacitated and, therefore, pitied. Leona not only paid their combined consequences, but bore the collective public scorn.

After media coverage of the case had died down and Leona had spent four years in jail, the court ruled that she had been unduly sentenced and duly punished. She was released to finish her sentence under house arrest while also putting in community-service hours. She reentered her life of luxury and sent her servants to do her community-service work. She had learned nothing. She "gets it" but doesn't care.

INSIGHTS

It's been said that if people like you, they'll forgive you anything, but if they don't like you, they are unforgiving to the fullest extent.

Charmers feel deserving and entitled to special allowances because of past, unavenged, injustices they've suffered or because of past success in getting away with similar behavior.

A Charmer needs to keep her audience fooled for protection. Leona made the mistake of insulting and abusing too many people, so she could no longer justify or hide her activities. A Charmer is usually smarter than that. Her arrogance concealed her paranoia until she was unmasked by outraged victims. Leona's private abuse was exposed, negating the belief and confidence in her public image.

Only when accountability is maintained does the whole past come to light. Once the charade is over, everything looks ugly. Though the public now knows the real Leona, it doesn't matter to her. After the temporary inconvenience of her time in prison, Leona has been able to land on her feet and continue to live comfortably and well.

Leona's motives and goals started out as a Charmer. The intervention of exposure did not lead to repentance, and she really could not plead ignorance as does a Charmer. At that point, she became a con artist. There was overwhelming evidence of her crimes. She continued to use the techniques of a Charmer, but she knew exactly what she had done, and she planned to change nothing. She felt justified in her actions because it satisfied her wants, and she felt no guilt. Leona was not skilled enough as a con artist to move on before being discovered.

Professor Smith

In the New England college town where he had come to teach, Professor Smith was a breath of fresh air. He seemed different from the other reserved, academic-type teachers in the university. He had kind eyes and a soft, caring demeanor. His tall and lanky frame was reminiscent of Gary Cooper. He was an effective teacher in the psychology department and very popular with his students.

In addition to instructing his classes in all the theories, methods, and techniques of counseling, Professor Smith specialized in guiding his students toward getting in touch with feelings—with their own as well as with their future clients'. He led them through countless exercises of role playing to help them experience how it would feel to suffer the loss of a child, a violent attack, the loss of a job, the infidelity of a spouse, and on and on. He encouraged his students' empathy and their tears.

The professor emphasized his students' need to work through their own "stuff" in order to be objective in their work and to avoid contaminating their future counseling practices. He was generous with his time in counseling students. When his intuition told him a student was in crisis, depressed, or hurting in some way, he would initiate contact with them, offering to help. His gentle gaze and comforting hug could melt even the most private, introverted person. But Professor Smith also used his knowledge of each student's vulnerabilities to make his selections for another purpose.

Everyone was so used to his sensitive behaviors, that it went unnoticed by most of them when he spent more time than usual with a woman. Only a few of the students, ones who had been around a while and who were ready to graduate, even gave a second thought to it. These veteran students had seen a pattern develop. It was the most attractive women (usually only one during each semester) who received special attention. These were usually obviously vulnerable individuals who were going through a difficult time.

Professor Smith needed to be in control and beneficent with women. He was the guru in his field of psychology, which was dominated by women and there were hundreds who thought he helped hang the moon. But he was seductive in private and had multiple infidelities with clients and students, many of which included sadomasochism. Even when there was no violence, he could seduce, throw away cruelly, and seduce again, repeating the cycle as long as possible to prove that he could.

In January, halfway through the academic year, Kathy transferred into the program from another of the state's universities. Kathy was a bright young woman, a no-nonsense, athletic, tomboy type, and she was happily married. Professor Smith was her advisor and was in the position of deciding which of the courses she had taken at the other university could transfer into his program. She was an honors student and already working in her field of study.

As Kathy sat down in the cafeteria with several seasoned classmates, she expressed to them her anger at the professor. He had not approved many of her courses, and now she would need another year to graduate.

One of the listeners suggested, "Go back to talk with him. This time, be sure to cry."

"Cry?" Kathy asked in horror. "I'm not going to cry! This is ridiculous. I have a letter from my former advisor outlining the courses I've had, which parallel courses here. He's just being arbitrary."

"Do you want to graduate on time?" someone else asked.

"Of course," said Kathy.

"Then cry!" was the unison response.

Just prior to their scheduled class time with Professor Smith the following week, Kathy saw the same group of students in the cafeteria. "It worked," she told them. "I hated doing it, but if that's his game, I have to play it. The minute I cried, he melted. He hugged me as I left his office and said, 'Friends?' I thought I was going to vomit."

Everyone laughed.

Other women hadn't been as fortunate as Kathy. Some had voluntarily poured out their hearts to him with one story or another. He had drawn them in with an unspoken acknowledgment of a special relationship: he was there for them alone. Most did not see the reality of their situation until later. But by then, they had graduated and moved on. Even though they saw him as a seducer and as abusing the power of his position, they just wanted it all behind them and did not want to bother making an issue of it.

His credibility in the community as a college professor and as a psychologist in a large, private practice convinced any critics, including faculty and administrators, that he was the victim of lovesick females—women he only had been trying to counsel. The professor would explain, persuasively and at length, the women's transference. Many of these women subsequently spent years in therapy, working through issues he had created in addition to their original problems (for which they received no help from him at all).

This all took place before the days of public policy on harassment and before lawsuits were a reality. Finally, however, a woman and her husband successfully sued Professor Smith for sexual harassment. The University asked him to retire early. He then moved to another state, where he has resumed his method of operation at another college. He will probably be more careful in his selection of women this time, but he needs his audience of admirers. It's doubtful he can stop himself. He may even be pushing for someone to stop him.

Profile

Jamie Smith was a high-school dropout. When he turned nineteen and was still struggling to get through his senior year, he gave up. The military was the only option he could see. On his first furlough, he married his childhood sweetheart, Nancy. She had graduated from high school with honors. Together they left for Alaska, where they stayed for his three years of service.

Nancy attended the local college and graduated early as a teacher. During those three years, Jamie had experimented with a class at the community college. He surprised himself by doing well. When he and Nancy returned home, Nancy began teaching, and Jamie tried school again. He finished his bachelor's degree in teaching. Then they both began their master's programs. While Nancy continued teaching and having children, Jamie taught and continued part-time graduate studies. He finished his Ph.D. without ever having earned a high-school diploma.

Jamie's struggle with the first twelve years of school was not because he couldn't perform academically. It was because of the bizarre home life in which he lived.

Jamie was the fourth son and last child born to a very unhappy woman. Her husband was in and out of her life, each time staying just long enough for her to become pregnant again. She had several miscarriages. By the time Jamie came along, the financial depravation his mother suffered (from lack of support from her husband) and the emotional disappointment of having no daughter was more than she could handle. Having one more active, rambunctious boy sent her over the edge.

Jamie was a beautiful baby with golden curls. His mother refused to cut his hair. She dressed him in the girl's clothes she had bought before he was born; she wanted this last child to be a girl. She even told friends and family that she had finally given birth to a girl. Until Jamie went to school, he was told he was a girl, was not allowed to change clothes in front of anyone (including his brothers), and was given girls' toys.

The school required Jamie's birth certificate for enrollment, and that was the beginning of his boyhood. The humiliation for Jamie and the adjustments for him, his family, and his friends were traumatic. His mother refused to accept that the secret was out. She continued to treat him like a girl. Jamie began leading a double life. He would periodically cut his own hair and live his real life outside the home. Only his mother was allowed to continue her fantasy.

As Jamie began to understand his situation, a seething rage began to develop. His became rebellious. As much as he needed his life at school and away from home, he refused to accept school authority figures and the demands they made on him. He was pushed along from grade to grade with little accomplishment. He never saw what he could do until he left home for good.

After what his mother had done to him, he could never feel good about women. Nancy was a year older than Jamie. She loved him from the time she met him in the tenth grade. She understood his struggles. That was enough for Jamie never to leave her, but not enough for him to remain faithful to her. She became a surrogate mother to him, one who would always forgive his boyish transgressions, a mother he needed to replace his own.

Nancy also represented the whipping post on which he took out the anger he felt toward his mother. The conflicting feelings he had for his mother, he began to project onto Nancy. Her self-defense was to live in denial, refusing to see, hear, or believe any of his infidelities. Jamie was a caring, loving husband and father. He just could not be with only one woman. Together he and Nancy played their game of pretense.

When Jamie was studying psychology, he began going to therapy himself. He came to a point of acceptance of his past, but he could not control the compulsions he had developed toward women. Instead, he managed them through living a dual existence.

Jamie and Nancy were getting close to their retirement when Jamie lost the lawsuit. They had to pay more than $100,000 out of their own pocket, over and above the amount paid by his professional liability insurance policy. At that point, denial was no longer an option for Nancy.

Jamie retired. His private practice began dwindling. By the time Nancy was able to retire two years later, they realized their only option was to move elsewhere and hope they could leave Jamie's past behind them. It's not likely.

INSIGHTS

The Charmer often comes from a very dysfunctional background. To cope, he may construct an active fantasy life in which he is the hero. There he can master anything and conquer anyone. Past injustices can be avenged.

A Charmer is skilled at selecting prospective admirers, and as an abuser, he is adept at selecting prospective victims. Victims become surrogates for people in his past who have hurt or disappointed him.

A Charmer will set up a situation, and when people respond naturally to it, he will point to their response as the issue or problem rather than what he did to provoke the response. When confronted, a Charmer is good at diverting attention away from himself while blaming the victims.

A Charmer will use kindly or loving gestures for the sole purpose of soliciting admiration or to avoid accountability.

Mark

Mark was popular in high school. He had good grades and a pseudomaturity for a teenage boy. Adults were impressed by the good-looking young man who knew where he was going and what he intended to accomplish. The parents of every girl he dated thought if their daughter could hitch her wagon to Mark's star, she would have a secure, wonderful life.

Cheryl was a pretty, blue-eyed girl with long, thick blond hair. She was shy, not as popular as Mark, and crazy about him. He hadn't noticed her until their senior year. When he realized how much she admired him, he was very impressed. His attention made her feel special. He would laugh at her jokes and quirks and flirtatiously tease her about her hobbies, her silliness, her appearance. Mark's continued attention to her made her more popular and more confident.

Mark took her with him to be around his friends and family to show her off to them, letting her know how proud of her he felt. When Cheryl took Mark to meet her family and friends, he was utterly charming and fascinating. However, after the initial meeting, he avoided further contact. Mark had such a busy social life that, though he often did not check with Cheryl in advance, she felt complimented when Mark automatically assumed she'd be with him. She felt honored, acceptable, and included.

Mark accompanied Cheryl to her church youth group, but he didn't feel comfortable with her friends, so they didn't go there anymore. He began to criticize and make fun of her family and friends in subtle, humorous ways. He was clever and subtle enough that it was impossible to accuse him of being unkind. This was the beginning of her isolation.

The time they spent with her family was brief. There was no quality time to really talk or interact. This ensured only a surface relationship for himself. To meet their obligations to Cheryl's family, he would invite them to his family gatherings, which kept him on his own turf and made him appear a wonderful person for including them all. After they were married, Cheryl saw it as one of Mark's clever means of controlling his environment and his image.

Other ways in which Mark managed to be the star without looking like he was out for positives strokes or attention was to select *the* place to take people, plan special surprises, and make sure all the prominent players were in attendance: business associates, special friends, or anyone he wanted to impress.

He had a way of delegating tasks to Cheryl for her to do the work and think it was her project, meanwhile he made all the suggestions and set up things to make himself look good. Cheryl was allowed to be the adoring, trophy wife who delighted in serving him. Her identity and praise came through making him look good.

Mark became the business success he predicted. In their high-roller, jet-setting lifestyle, he became more demanding of Cheryl. Her appearance had to be perfect. He guided her in the way she dressed, wore her hair, and even her choice of what to drink or eat when they were out in public. He chided her for gaining a pound over her teenage figure, while his girth grew steadily with the years. He set her up for failure again and again. For example, he gave her no advance information about new clients they'd be seeing, but he would berate her at the end of the evening for things she'd said.

She was never allowed to discuss their children, even if someone asked about them. Mark almost acted ashamed of having children. Also, Cheryl dared never to use the children as an excuse for not being constantly available when he needed her. Mark was a totally uninvolved father when it came to his son and two daughters. When Mark was at home, the tension they all felt was inhibiting. The children were afraid of him. There was no fun or laughter when he was there. From time to time, however, he would repeat some story he had disinterestedly endured hearing from Cheryl about the children, garnering great mileage with his audience and enhancing his public image.

His entire life was geared toward business. The family grew accustomed to living without him most of the time. In Mark's mind, he provided handsomely for them, and they should be grateful and make no demands of him. Mark and Cheryl both drove Jaguars, but money problems left Cheryl clipping coupons and buying the children's and her clothes at K-Mart.

Evidence began to appear of affairs, fraud, and cocaine use. Mark's financial overextension led to bankruptcy, loss of their $600,000 California home, problems with the IRS that went on for years, and alienation from friends and family. Cheryl had ignored her growing inner pain and embarrassment. She remained his loyal believer and defender. Mark had lulled her into a glow of safety and a belief in his ability to handle things and make choices for them.

Her moment of truth came in a confrontation with Mark's latest girlfriend. Cheryl discovered Mark was paying the girlfriend's rent in an expensive apartment and that he would frequently take her children there. Cheryl's discovery came as her home was being sold and she had gone back to work to pay Mark's debts, which included a sizable amount to his drug dealer.

Mark's response was that he had nothing to hide, that this woman was merely a friend, and that Cheryl's imagination was running away with her. He suggested that Cheryl was really "losing it" to believe these things. He was asking her to not believe her own eyes in seeing the canceled checks for the woman's apartment and expensive gifts. He was asking Cheryl to not believe her own ears as even Mark's friends and coworkers were beginning to tell Cheryl the truth.

Mark's lies became harder to believe. He still tried to use work to cover his habit of breaking grandiose promises to his family. Cheryl no longer accepted his assertions that all he was doing was for her and the children. His arguments were circular. Cheryl finally saw that either Mark was a very sick liar or that she was in total delusion. Although she was reeling from the blows of her new awareness, she had enough self-respect to trust her own judgment at this point.

As she fought back, she turned his own arguments against him and began using his techniques for herself. She reproached herself with *How stupid could you have been all these years?* She gave him ultimatums about his behavior. He had a limited time to clean up his life or face divorce. Mark was totally unprepared for her emerging strength. At first he tried to woo her back in line as he had always been able to do. When that failed and he saw she was serious, he sold what they had left and moved the family across country to be near his family. He even took her to see her family for the holidays, something she had not been able to do for years.

Mark told her he had paid off all the debts and had settled things with the IRS. He announced he was buying a new business. This time, she was going to be working with him. They would be partners together in their new venture. He included some family members to work in the new organization. Mark didn't think they should buy another house until the business was established.

Cheryl and the children were settled into an apartment, Cheryl was working in the business, and Mark had to go back to California to tie up loose ends. His trips became more and more frequent. His involvement in the new business was less and less. His behavior again became erratic. Now he had her at a distance, entrenched in the new business so she could not hinder his doing whatever he pleased. His absence from the business and his withdrawal of funds for operation led to failure of the new business and left Cheryl feeling responsible. Mark made sure she continued in that belief.

Cheryl was distraught and immobilized. She knew they were living separate lives in distance as well as in fact. Away from the superficial lifestyle and friends they had always had around them, and without Mark constantly telling her what she should and shouldn't believe, Cheryl began to awaken from her twenty-year sleep.

The family who worried about her and missed her all those years became visible to Cheryl again. Her parents insisted she seek therapy, and since they were supporting her and her children, she didn't think she should refuse.

During Cheryl's first session in counseling, her therapist asked, "What causes you to allow yourself to be treated this way and call it okay?"

Cheryl could not claim some horrible family or dysfunctional upbringing. She'd had a happy childhood and loving parents and extended family. She had felt confident as a child and had been content, until Mark entered her life. As a teenager, she had no way of seeing Mark as a user of people. She had no way of predicting how he would become caught up in his own ambition and sense of privilege.

As the truth was unveiled in her recovery process, her anger sat firmly on the surface of her mind. It provided the motivation she needed to get away from Mark and to get her children away from his influence. When Cheryl began the divorce action, Mark resumed his pattern of romancing her, as he had always done if she disagreed with him. This time, though, even Mark saw it would not work. But he still wanted her back where she belonged!

The divorce took almost three years. Mark fought it, running up extensive lawyer fees. It was revealed that Mark had never settled his debts. He showed the court his bankruptcy to establish a minimum child support requirement. Their property and all assets were gone.

Cheryl settled to escape being a partner in his remaining debts. She was resigned to her limited lifestyle and rearing her children alone. Cheryl knew she could never count on Mark for child support. He would keep her tied up in court spending more money to chase him and force him to pay than she would ever collect.

The amazing thing to Cheryl was how free she felt, how content with her little apartment and her three beautiful, healthy children. Life was opening up to Cheryl—her own life, not one she lived through Mark. Mark never could allow that.

Mysteriously, he was again making $200,000 a year, buying luxury items, taking exotic vacations with his girlfriend, and living in grand style. The most important thing in Cheryl's life, other than Mark, had been her children. They were now teenagers, and Mark began luring them away from their mother, giving them their own cars and the lifestyle they previously had known. He also threatened no support for college if they did not live with him.

He was very kind about it all. He convinced the children that it would lighten the burden for their mother since she could not make very much money. The children were never told about the child-support issue, which had made their lives with their mother so financially difficult. So Mark looked like a hero, rescuing them and their mother.

Since the children had so little time with their dad growing up, they were torn between leaving their mother and the opportunity to have their father's full attention. They would be living in their old neighborhood with their old friends. Besides, Dad promised them they could visit their mother often. What he didn't say was that Cheryl would have to pay the airfare from California to Maryland for the three of them to visit her. She is able to afford it only once a year. Cheryl also pays for any phone calls from her children.

Since the bankruptcy, Mark had set up ways around showing his income. He petitioned the court for child-support payments from Cheryl, and he had the money to enforce it.

Mark's child rearing is done loosely. One of the children has a learning disability. Cheryl had spent a great deal of time with him and had arranged for tutors to help him keep up with his class. While the boy was in Mark's care, that help was gone. The son failed to graduate from high school.

Mark's ego can't handle that. He has become abusive to the boy. Over the years prior to his son's failure to graduate, Mark would never allow his son to reap any natural consequences for his behavior. Mark would artificially prop up his boy to look successful in athletics and academics. Those efforts are no longer possible. Sadly, his son's confidence level is so low now that he believes he cannot support himself.

The other two children have come to realize the truth of their situation, and they see what has happened to their brother. They are near graduation from high school and feel trapped into going along with their dad in order to get what they need from him financially.

Cheryl has grown and is emotionally healthy again. Her heart aches for her children, in not having them with her and in seeing what they are experiencing with their dad. She consoles herself with the thought that she no longer has to cover for Mark. She hasn't had to be the "bad guy" in telling her children about him. They are learning the truth firsthand

Cheryl worries they will become like Mark. Her faith in herself and in them reminds her that the children are hers as well as Mark's and that she was their greatest influence in their most formative years. She knows she did her best for them. She trusts that and she has forgiven herself.

Profile

Mark was the oldest son, followed by a brother and two sisters. He led the way for the other children. If there had been a program in his elementary school for gifted and talented children, he would have been part of it. His siblings were average in every way that Mark was outstanding. Mark was a take-charge male like his father. His brother and sisters were followers like their mother. From the time he became aware of his specialness, he learned to maximize it to get ahead of others.

The fact that he was also a beautiful child made it easy for others to give in to him and grant him extra privileges. Mark was a born leader and achieved every honor possible in school. He was not required to do chores at home since he was so involved in his own worthwhile activities. He enjoyed his "perfect" image, and never tarnished it until he went away to college. There Mark began to relax somewhat and to explore.

He was picked to join the top fraternity on campus. He was bright enough to maintain good grades (barely the Dean's List) and yet indulge himself in the freedom of distance from home. He partied with the best of them. He had convinced Cheryl to attend the same school. While at college, Mark learned how to cheat on Cheryl and keep it from her. He knew his dad had done the same thing. He was always told how much he was like his dad, so why shouldn't he do it too? Mark also introduced Cheryl to his drinking and recreational drug use. Those were things he learned on his own, apart from his father.

Mark was not at the top of his class when he graduated, but his personality put him at the top of every company interviewer's list. He landed a top job with a large organization, which would give him unlimited opportunities for advancement. He was on his way.

Cheryl and Mark were married between his junior and senior year of college. Cheryl had dropped out of school to work as a secretary to support them. She never finished college until after their divorce. Mark applied for and was granted a transfer across country to California. There they were far away from both families and free to live a whole new life.

It wasn't long before they had greatly surpassed their lower middle-income families. For the first few years, their relatives were in awe of them. They told themselves the reason they heard from Cheryl and Mark so seldom was because of the great demand on their time created by Mark's job.

As the years went by, it became clear that Cheryl and Mark were avoiding everything in their former life. For Cheryl's family, it seemed she was lost to them forever. They didn't know her anymore, and they didn't know her children at all. To them it appeared that Cheryl wanted it that way. They couldn't know the emotional erosion she was enduring. She was lonely and exhausted. She was also ashamed.

Cheryl was on a treadmill, playing mother, father, tutor, and Barbie-doll hostess. She had no time to think or feel. Her dance card was full.

Mark felt nothing. He just plunged headlong into a candy land of thrills and things. He was oblivious to anyone else's opinions or feelings. His assumption was that his family was riding on his coattail. The expansion of the liberties he took grew ever easier. Once he grabbed the tail of the success comet, he never looked back, and he never could hear any voices calling after him.

Mark knew no one at any depth. The only people he had any time or energy for were the ones clearing the way for him. No one was more surprised than Mark when his life began to crumble. He believed he was in total control of his realm and everything in it.

Cheryl's rebellion was a nuisance to Mark. It interfered with his agenda and distracted him. She had always handled things so that he could enjoy his freedom to do as he pleased. Though he told himself that everything he did was for her and the kids, it was really all for himself and about himself.

The divorce caused Mark to feel scared. He was out of control. If Cheryl could no longer be managed, what else might be in danger of escaping? When he couldn't put his marriage back together, he hated her. As far as he was concerned, Cheryl had caused all this. Her place was with him in the ideal life! He would have to punish her for destroying what they'd had together and for tarnishing *his* image.

The timing of the bankruptcy worked in his favor. He used it to avoid sharing any assets with her. He managed to keep her from having anything without him. Mark's ultimate vengeance was to take the children out of Cheryl's reach. It would also help him to feel no guilt.

INSIGHTS

The Charmer uses family and friends as a smoke screen to cover his tracks and to divert attention away from any misbehavior.

The Charmer takes full advantage of the love others have for him. He demands that it be unconditional approval of his behavior.

The Charmer is adept at laying heavy guilt trips on anyone who confronts him about his bad behavior. He will lie about what he's done and try to shame others for believing such things about him.

The Charmer turns circumstances around to make others believe they are inadequate in their love, loyalty, or ability to see truth.

The threat of abandonment is particularly frightening to the Charmer. He fears he might cease to exist. If he cannot persuade you to stay, he will threaten you if you leave.

SOAPBOX CHARMERS:
EXAMPLES FROM
THE POLITICAL ARENA

Because we choose our politicians to run our country, we allow them to make choices for us—choices that greatly impact our lives. We give them permission to take money from us and to decide how to spend it. We let them make rules and laws by which we must abide, and we submit to punishment from them if we disobey these laws. When it comes to politics, we trust them to know more about the big picture than we do, and we believe they will make conscientious decisions for our good.

A breach of their promises or integrity (especially if it is after the fact and we've already suffered grave consequences) leads to the erosion of our sense of safety and hope. We lose confidence in our own ability to make good decisions. The feeling of having participated in our own demise—whether financial, economic, or personal—debilitates and demoralizes the human spirit. It shakes our belief in others and in the world around us, along with our confidence in ourselves.

With a Charmer in charge, it takes a long time before we figure things out. They are so sincere, so convincing. Their sense of those things in which we want to believe and their great repertoire of slogans and phrases mesmerize us.

It's no wonder the founding fathers did not create a pure democracy but rather a republic—a representative government. We do not have majority rule. The majority quite often is wrong, easily swept away with the moment, and can develop a mob or herd mentality. Instead, we try to elect the best educated, the best thinkers, the best qualified representatives of our interests. We trust them to maintain a level head, to make legal rather than emotional decisions, and to do what is best for the country as a whole, regardless of the popularity or sentiment of the moment.

Many will never believe the reality when a Charmer is exposed. It is depressing to discover you have invested years in a wrong direction. It is also embarrassing. People would rather live in denial than admit they have been fooled or used. They resent the idea of the time and energy it would take to deal with the problem were it carried to its logical conclusion.

The business of government, however, is not a passive exercise for those governed. Giving up individual freedoms to a governing body for the purpose of long-term good for the whole requires involvement, awareness, and careful attention. Checks and balances are our best insurance.

Eva Peron

Eva Peron became the most powerful and influential woman in the history of South America and one of the world's most powerful and influential women of the twentieth century. From the age of fifteen, Eva Marie Duarte—a poor, pretty girl from Argentina—began seducing and using men to climb a ladder of fame and security. Each successive man in her life was wealthier and more powerful than the last. Her quest ended when she finally captured the heart of Argentina's emerging political star Colonel Juan Peron.

By the time Eva met the older, widowed army officer, she had slept her way from her beginnings in a small town all the way to having status as a model and then as an actress of some reputation in Buenos Aires. The handsome Juan Peron had been the Minister of Labor, endearing himself to the workers, the masses of Argentina. In addition to their attraction to each other, they shared a ruthless ambition for fame and leadership. Eva's identification with the workers gave the two of them a further bond that became their ticket to years of hero worship.

"I am one of you," Eva would say to the people.

Eva became Peron's mistress. When he lost favor with the governing regime and was arrested, she stood by him. When the people demanded his release, the two created one of many myths that would emerge about Eva, saying that she had been the one to rally the people to protest for Peron.

Eva and Juan not only loved and trusted each other, they loved their common desire for power and notoriety. They shared a goal of leading the country. Peron married his mistress, an unusual move for a member of the upper class. The two campaigned successfully to make Juan Peron the country's president. Eva seized her position as first lady with great presumption. She began to create a new image of herself, befitting a first lady. She spent money lavishly for designer clothes, jewels, and furs, establishing herself as the jewel of Argentina.

She became constantly visible to the masses, involving herself in every public forum possible. She was the first woman to do so. This created a furor among the men in the government. Machismo is the primary identity of South American men, particularly among the upper class and the military. The idea of a woman leading them in anything is repugnant to them.

Eva used her position as a platform for feminism, securing voting rights for women. Her purpose was less for the advancement of women than for channeling their gratitude into additional votes and support for her husband. She was Peron's strongest spokesperson, a one-woman public relations force. She deferred to him, praised him. She was ensuring her own security through his security in the presidency.

Alongside that, she began building her own following who saw her as a benevolent saint, the humble wife of their great leader. She was a greater actress than she had been given credit for during her acting-career days. By playing her role as one who bowed to the will of the people, she endeared herself to them as no one else in their history had. In truth, she orchestrated everything. She set up the role she wanted to play, but she managed to lead her followers to believe it was their idea and their dream.

The power of her position allowed Eva to take revenge on all those who had hurt or rejected her over the years. If the upper class did not pay her the homage she expected and believed she deserved, she cut them out of the scene. People who had rejected her professionally and who had not fully appreciated her were excommunicated from her social circle, as well as from the circles of anyone who wanted to stay in Eva's realm.

Eva became a female Robin Hood in Argentina. She managed to extort money from the rich to build hospitals, to provide housing, and to supply food for the poor. If the wealthy refused to donate what she asked, their businesses would be hounded by inspectors for safety or sanitary violations.

She gave personal attention to the people. She interviewed and granted favors for thousands of people through her charitable projects. It is estimated she secured $50 million a year for the purpose of helping the workers. No one is sure; she never kept records. It didn't seem to matter to the masses if she took some for herself. They were living better than they imagined possible.

She walked among them. She greeted and hugged them. She promoted herself and them. She gathered as much publicity as she could manage. Her message to the people was, "I made it. You can too. I dress and live this way as an example for you to follow, to believe in. I do this for you!" They bought it. They delighted in and were proud of her glamour and position in Argentina and in the world. They fulfilled many of their own fantasies through her.

To the workers she became a saint, an angel, their fairy godmother. They affectionately called her Evita, the Lady of Hope. She stirred great emotion among them. She could whip her audience into an emotional frenzy as no one else could, and she could keep them there. Evita and Juan Peron had no children. Politics was their child. The people of Argentina were their family.

The power of their supporters squashed any opposition. When the Peron fiscal irresponsibility finally led to economic disaster for the country, Juan and Eva took over the newspapers and touted Evita's popularity as a diversion. Eva buoyed their reign for a while longer until she became terminally ill with cancer. Rather than slow her pace to prolong her life, however, she continued her obsession of promoting and ensuring Juan's reelection as well as her new image as a martyr. She lived and died for her position of adoration and power.

By the end of their reign, the Perons had stripped the once-wealthy Argentina of most of its treasury.

Profile

Childhood shame and rejection marked Eva Marie Duarte's life forever. She was the fifth illegitimate child born to her mother and a wealthy landowner. The stigma of living in the shadows of her father's other, legitimate family, became the motivation for Eva to seek her own legitimacy by whatever means possible.

Eva and her family had her father's name, and everyone in their town knew about them. When her father died, however, Eva and her family were not allowed to attend his funeral. The insult of that rebuff never left her. She hated the upper class for their power over her.

As soon as she finished puberty, she seduced the first man who could take her to the city where she could get started in her retribution. She used her beauty and charm to entice one man after another, men who would support her financially and introduce her to the contacts she needed to become independent of anyone else's power.

For the rest of her life, to all those not beguiled by her, she would be known as a whore, regardless of anything else she did or achieved. That part of her past she could never escape. What she could do, however, was flaunt the power of her position in their faces and exercise power over their lives whenever she had the opportunity. That need never left her. It was the driving force of her existence, her obsession.

Juan Peron was one more rung on the ladder she was climbing. He was the top. Eva's love and devotion to him increased with each new layer of their relationship. He was old enough to be her father. He adored her. When he married her, he bestowed on her the legitimacy she craved. It was a gift her own father never gave her.

The gift reached far beyond mere legitimacy as a wife. The marriage offered Eva more than just having a husband. For her, it legitimized her whole life and carried the prestige of sharing his position and his work. It provided her with an acceptable and praiseworthy opportunity also to *give* a gift that would have great value.

Eva was not just a beautiful asset to Juan Peron's presidency, she became the reason he was able to stay in power. Her husband knew and appreciated this. This present laid at his feet endeared Eva to him for life.

Regardless of Eva's love and devotion to her husband, though, she was even more devoted to herself. By taking good care of him, she was taking good care of herself. His security was her security. One wonders if she would have spent all the influence she had on his career if she, as a woman, could have been the president of the country. Her inner fears of dependency were always alive.

At the pinnacle of her popularity, she planted the idea in the minds of the people that she should be vice president. As they chanted their call to her, she played out her part and humbly bowed to their will. The military and government officials knew there was the possibility Juan Peron would die in office. He was getting old. That could leave Eva in charge of them and the country. Their machismo could not tolerate that. They rebelled.

Once again, Eva was forced to bow to masculine power over her. It was not just the power of men but also of the upper class: the two elements she had resented since childhood. Regardless of the height of her success, she could not overpower all men or all of the aristocracy.

Eva used even her illness to perpetuate her illusion of martyrdom and sainthood. Her humility and popularity carried more weight than any political position. Rather than reveal the loss of her power struggle to become vice president, she saved face by citing her illness as the reason she would need to sacrifice that position. Evita was a master at writing her own script and a genius at manipulating a whole country to play their roles for her own purpose.

Her extravagant lifestyle as first lady outshone any of the aristocracy. During her reign, she executed great power over them. In the end, however, they stood between her and the last rung on the ladder of her ambition.

INSIGHTS

Charmers usually have an unconscious hatred for the opposite sex. Their method of camouflage is to become especially attractive to that sex. Their purpose is to use that attraction to conquer them.

The Charmer feels powerless and out of control of her own life. She seeks to erase those feelings by gaining control over others or over situations she considers threatening.

The Charmer has a poor self-image and a feeling of inadequacy. These deficiencies become her project, and her obsession is to change them. She will use her attractiveness and charm to convince others of her worth. She believes her reflection in their eyes will convince herself as well.

The Charmer feels justified in doing whatever she must to provide the security and love she desperately needs.

The Charmer believes she deserves special allowances and treatment as payment for past injustices.

The Charmer believes her own publicity.

The more grandiose the Charmer's dreams and aspirations, the deeper the level of pathology and the greater the danger to her victims.

Bill Clinton

On February 12, 1998, the *Wall Street Journal* devoted a full page to chronicle the events surrounding the Clinton presidency, from shortly after he took office in 1993. The title was "Obstruction and Abuse: A Pattern." The page was done in small print, subdivided into blocks of dates and details about all the questionable characters and events connected to Bill Clinton. A sidebar offered (for just $39.95 plus shipping) a *three-volume* set called "A Journal Briefing: White-water," containing the full history of the Clinton scandals.[11]

This respected publication of long-standing is only one of many of its caliber to research and investigate the man and his practices. Reams of paper from an entire forest have been used to chart the meteoric rise of Bill Clinton along with the lies, inconsistencies, stonewalling, and slippery-quick exits from suspicious situations by this president and his league of supporters and cohorts. It isn't necessary to recite the details of his career here.

This tall, attractive, personable, Southern "good ole boy" is a genius wordsmith and inventive communicator. His confidence and ambition put him at the top of everything on which he set his sights. His brilliant strategies and natural people skills are like cream, always rising to the top. On the occasions he has encountered roadblocks, they were eventually pushed out of the way, developing further his reputation from childhood as "the comeback kid." He would never give up on anything he wanted. He would take great risks, playing the odds that he'd win sometimes and at least get close to the other times. Even when he came in second in a race, he considered it a strategic success. He had made his mark for the next time.

The *Wall Street Journal* article cited one incident after another (during the Clinton invasion of Washington) of Clinton cronies propelled into key positions, casting aside long-serving employees, including some in the high offices of the Justice Department. Many of Clinton's gang had been or soon were indicted on various charges of fraud, embezzlement, intimidation of foes, and bribery. Some became felons, were sent to prison, or died mysteriously.

Clinton has been part of each link of a chain, including those involving sex scandals with numerous women; the misuse of his office as governor of Arkansas and president of the United States to secure and facilitate his sexual misconduct; the misuse of FBI files against political opponents; disappearance of documents; Nannygate; Travelgate; Pantygate; campaign finance abuses, some of which may have compromised our country's values and national security; and on and on.

Again and again, this chain was hurled to drive good people out of their jobs. Many who would not enlist in the Clinton army were forced to resign from their positions of government service in protest, all to no avail.

Again and again, the artful dodger would stall response, distort the truth, or distract attention away from real issues. If the protests continued or were loud enough, the Clinton camp went on the offensive to discredit the messenger. Their consistent method of operation was a strong offense as their only defense.

Over the years, Clinton developed a reputation as "Slick Willie" and "The Teflon President." He would ignore critics as though they were invisible and as if he were invincible. He would walk and talk with utter confidence, always appearing presidential or even regal as though he had won the presidential race by a landslide instead of by default. Like most Charmers and con artists, Clinton always manages to be in the right place at the right time for the best advantage or lucky break.

As one news analyst observed, Clinton has been running for office all his life. He's always out campaigning for his next election or venture. He has spent very little time in his office actually doing.

His forté is working the people and public opinion. He is a master at gathering publicity and making everything he does a promotional opportunity. He is particularly skilled at turning around the many self-inflicted disasters and scandals in his life to work for his advantage.

Clinton's charisma enlisted a devoted entourage who would ride his train to power. Their belief in him and in his manifest destiny justified whatever means required for their end goal. Many, such as James Carville, whose "pit bull attacks" on the Clinton administration's opposition, look increasingly ridiculous in their continued defense of indefensible acts.

Clinton uses those who believe in him for his own agenda, regardless of the cost to those individuals. He cunningly seduces them into ignoring fact or testimony, and he does it all, believing it is his right to do so. Regardless of the burden on his friends, family, and others, Clinton has no shame, no embarrassment, no remorse, and no real repentance. He is actually a tragic, shame-based character who attempts to hide his shame by behaving shamelessly.

The beginning of his presidency was next to a disaster. His first impression in Washington was less than wonderful. The establishment was not as easily bowled over by Clinton as were the hometown folks in his native Arkansas. Two years into his term, the electorate revealed its disapproval in the rejection of Democrats, electing a Republican Congress.

Clinton is torn between ambition and idealism. He has an instinctive ability to tell people what they want to hear and to pick issues that reflect the most idealism and popularity, whether right or wrong, practical or impractical, good or not good for the general constituency.

After the first two disappointing years of his term, Clinton's reaction was to run with his strong suit: playing to the people. He projected an image of being a moderate: a man of the people in contrast to President George Bush's image as a Washington elitist and Ross Perot's image of a wealthy man trying to buy the presidency. He used his anti-Washington establishment, Baby Boomer-generation image to incite the public to see him as one of them. He would be the first president born after World War II, and he personified the romantic, American movie-hero loner who "did it *his* way."

He moved his politics toward the middle. On occasion, Clinton stole thunder from Republicans by using popular parts of their platform to claim as his idea before the American people. The claims of accomplishment he made were only achieved once he cooperated with his new Congress. In his typical Ted Kennedy leadership style, he felt the public pulse, endeared himself to causes of various powerful factions, stepped out in front, and invited, "Follow me!" He then took credit for being the great innovator.

Even if he was wrong or controversial, he impressed people with his rhetoric and stalwart stand on his position. In that area, he emulated his hero John Kennedy and became the people's new hero. Even his speech style and patterns are copies of the former president and his brothers.

It didn't matter to the masses what he did or didn't do. Like Kennedy, Clinton is a master of charm. He has a repertoire of smiles, clever stories, feigned empathy, and humor.

Kennedy had more class in hiding his indiscretions and inadequacies. (The press was also more discreet and forgiving at the time of Kennedy's reign.) Clinton openly distorts, deceives, and assassinates the reputations of anyone not on his bandwagon. Bill Clinton has managed to raise troubleshooting, bimbo management, spin doctoring, and damage control to a real art form.

Even when his deeds were exposed to the light, Clinton continued to successfully persuade his followers to accept and even applaud "dumbing down" and compromising the office of President of the

United States. He has become a bad joke, and he has shamed the office he held. None of that matters to him, as long as he hangs on to what *he* wants: a place in history books. However, his legacy will be vastly different from his original plan.

Over the years, Clinton has become blatant and arrogant in believing he could always manage to con his way out of situations. He's very good at it, but he finally was confronted by others of equal intelligence and determination and who were better lawyers than he.

His defenders use circular arguments to defend Clinton and themselves for continuing to trust him. They openly deny evidence to the contrary. They are rude in their arguments, loud and insulting to anyone who challenges them with truth. For his continuing believers away from the Washington Beltway, the distance promotes their fantasy.

People don't like to admit they've bought into a farce. It takes great ego strength to face and admit you've been conned. Those who invest so heavily in a particular person or cause usually do not have great ego strength. That's why they fall so hard and so deep. They would rather go on defending their choice, like faithful codependents, pretending they don't look foolish, than to suffer the embarrassment of admitting they were sucked in. However, like victims of so many other Charmers, victims of Bill Clinton only prolong their own misery by delaying acceptance of their situation.

Profile

As a "daughter of the South," it is my observation that southern men usually fall into one of two categories: either that of the "Southern gentleman" or the "good ole boy." The gentleman is not only charming but also excels in good manners, graciousness, and true appreciation of others. The good ole boy can be charming or obnoxious, but he has a distinct attitude of presumption. His attitude determines his behaviors and the outcome.

The good ole boy will develop automatically in the absence of positive examples or specific teaching to become a gentleman. Self-centered, self-serving, and exploitative, these men are adolescents in grown-up bodies. Rules are a nuisance to them and are seen as things to be stretched or broken. Good ole boys are cocky exhibitionists. They become Charmers and con artists.

Gentlemen are the product of consistent role models and instruction. They serve others equally as they serve their own needs. They are appropriately sacrificial at times. Their goal is to do the right thing with the right intention. Honor is their hallmark. Virtue is their reward.

Honor and virtue are things Bill Clinton talks about easily. They are noble words his public wants to hear. He is good with idealistic, inspiring words and grandiose ideas, but he doesn't know how to live them. He's full of talk about values, but he doesn't have a clue as to their real meaning or execution.

The biggest loss in Bill Clinton's life was in the erroneous messages he gleaned from growing up. The role models and the general philosophy of life to which Bill was exposed through his mother gave him his sense of entitlement, a belief that he could do as he pleased regardless of anyone or anything. He learned to rationalize his choices and behaviors to best others. He learned to admire the people who held the power, no matter how they'd gotten it. He was determined to get it too.

Clinton's early life was marked by major losses. His father died before he was born. His mother left him with her parents for several years while she left the state to work. Even with loving grandparents and a legitimate reason for the absence of parents, a child naturally would feel abandoned.

Those who knew young Bill back then say the loss of a father greatly impacted his life. No doubt the loss of his mother during his formative years was even more devastating. Since she was his only parental role model, her example carried a double impact. She was the example her son followed, and she was the person he turned out to be like. In place of multiple marriages, Bill had multiple affairs.

Bill took charge of his life with the determination and toughness of a survivor. When his mother returned for him when he was about age ten, it was with a new husband—the second of several she would have. Bill's new stepfather drank heavily and was abusive to the family. Bill inherited his mother's love of fun and excitement and her live-for-today attitude. She was a party girl. She did her own thing and apologized to no one for it.

Through his parents' associations, Bill grew up with constant exposure to local back-room politics and to wheeling and dealing in business in Hot Springs, Arkansas, a haven for big-city gangsters. His was a corrupt environment.

Behind Bill's charm, skilled rhetoric, and easygoing style was a calculating young leader-in-the-making who could turn anything to his advantage. With a mother who never corrected her children's misdeeds nor issued any consequences, Bill and his younger half-brother, Roger, embarked on lives of instant gratification with little restraint or conscience. Roger followed in his dad's footsteps, adding a drug problem to the mix of alcohol and abusing his mother.

Bill Clinton is driven by his dysfunctional background. He is a classic example and the worst product of a childhood with alcoholism and codependency. In adulthood, he has been bright enough to continue avoiding the consequences of his actions. His plans for success at any cost were watered and grew in a part of the country too gracious, or perhaps too naive, to stop him.

The small-town city of Hot Springs and the simple life he'd known could not contain Bill Clinton's ambitions or satisfy his immense dreams. He needed to rise above his upbringing. He wanted to test his metal in a prestigious part of the country and attend a respected school. From the day he hit Georgetown University, he used his

Southern charm to begin a personal campaign to become known and liked, enough to win the presidency of the freshman class.

The next step up was to work for the respected Senator Fulbright. He applied for and was granted a Rhodes scholarship to study abroad. Bill became an instant local celebrity and gained even more special privileges. He was continuing his move uptown. A big interference in his journey was the threat of being drafted during the Vietnam War.

The sequence of events in which Clinton rationalized his decision and managed to escape the draft helped hide his real reason for not wanting to serve. Two of his close friends had died there. Clinton arrogantly believed that the bright, gifted young people (such as he) who were the future of America should not waste their lives in Vietnam. He was a true product of the havoc of the sixties.

For graduate school, in keeping with many of the other Rhodes scholars he had met in England, he chose Yale Law School. It was not because he wanted to be a lawyer, but rather for the contacts he could make there and for the networking possibilities. His goal was politics.

At Yale he met the second important woman in his life who would prove to be his best enabler: Hillary Rodham. She was quite a prize. Not only was she as bright and as accomplished as he, but also she had already earned the respect of peers and mentors. Hillary was hard working and more controlled about her life than Bill was, which would complement his style and make life easier for him. She could do the work while he dazzled the voters with his personality. But most important, she deeply loved him, believed in him, and sacrificed her own future career for his.

Her devotion would validate him, make him look good, and keep him floating on top of the water of, perhaps, a bigger pond than the one to which he was accustomed. She was his trophy—one valuable enough to need and to want not to lose, but not valuable enough to be enough. He knew her well, and he knew her devotion to him and her forgiving capacity of his indiscretions.

It doesn't matter how smart or accomplished a woman is, she can be conned like anyone else. If she's head over heels in love, she will sacrifice everything for that relationship. Sadly, if the object of her affection is a Charmer or con artist, she will forever be carrying the relationship all by herself. What Hillary doesn't understand is what she's married to or how woefully incapable her husband is of loving anyone but himself. Like anyone else in his life, she is a vehicle for his success. Vehicles are only allowed in a Charmer's life if they stay totally committed and are willing to continue in their denial that it is a one-sided union.

Clinton knew he had to start his political career in a safe place: back home. He entered politics when the Democratic Party was losing its power. He took his new wife back to Arkansas and taught law school until the time was right to try a run for office. He lost his first election, which was a long shot anyway. But his goal was to make a name for himself, which he was able to do just by trying. He succeeded in becoming the attorney general, and in that position, he used the spotlight, taking up high-profile causes, adding to his notoriety. At age thirty-two, he became the youngest governor of Arkansas.

The arrogance he exhibited in his first term alienated the Arkansas powerbrokers. Instead of appointing local supporters who helped elect him, he brought in his new friends from up North. He tried to put a new, laid-back, antiestablishment face on the traditional, patriotic, old-guard Arkansas State House. Clinton violated their value of "dancing with the one that brought you." Once again, as they say in the South, "He got above his raisin'." He lost the next election.

Clinton was appropriately humbled. To get back into the people's good graces and to pick up where he'd left off in his political career, he apologized, validated their decision to turn him out, and applauded their graciousness in giving him a second chance. This time, he would dance with the right people for four more terms as their governor.

The lessons he learned through that experience would stay with him from then on. Thereafter, he has made sure he properly showed his appreciation for his backers. He learned how much he needed them and what assets they could become. He discovered how willing they were to risk breaking the law, to risk losing their reputations, and to live in denial in order to hang onto his brass ring.

Life on the edge with someone such as Bill Clinton is a dynamic adventure. Like sky diving, racing, or any number of high-thrill activities, a person can go so fast that he misjudges his limitations and underestimates the price of the ticket. Crashing can be a fatal surprise.

Clinton became a big fish in the little pond of Arkansas. Except for advances in education, he was primarily known for his personality. In association with other governors throughout the country, as usual, his charisma won him new stature and the promise of an entrance into national politics.

His brazen grandstanding at the Democratic Convention in 1988 drew boos from the crowd. As usual, he turned it into a huge publicity success for himself with an appearance on the *Tonight Show*. Thus began his campaign with the American public for national office.

INSIGHTS

Charmers and con artists use the divide-and-conquer technique. This is very effective in taking the attention and the heat off themselves. They get others distracted and focusing on minor things or fighting among themselves.

Charmers twist the truth, lie, distract, accuse, and use irrational and irrelevant arguments if confronted. They are adept at turning the tables to cast doubt on any accuser's motive and credibility, regardless of and avoiding any facts. Their inconsistency between what they say and what they do keeps others off guard and unable to quickly respond in a healthy manner.

The Charmer often uses sex as a means of control, whether to withhold it or to demand it more frequently or in a bizarre fashion that is not mutually fulfilling or agreed upon. A man may even withhold his own ejaculation, even though he goes to great length to satisfy his partner. The Charmer enjoys knowing he can captivate someone, going right up to the point of connection, only to walk away, leaving the other person forever hopeful but never successful. The Charmer needs to know he could be involved if he chose to, but at the same time, he does not want to risk full involvement. It's a game for him.

Charmers are missing a sense of healthy shame, so they have no problem facing people after offending someone or creating a mess.

Charmers are persistent, but not in the sense of the healthy kind of perseverance needed to accomplish a difficult task. Theirs is a desperate need to not accept "no." The strategy is to outlast the objections or protests of anyone in the way, believing the other person will grow weary or be caught off guard and their resistance will end. It doesn't appear, at the time, to be that important to the victim, but once the victim begins giving in, the fly is in the spider's web, and the game accelerates.

Charmers need to know their charm can work on anyone they might choose, male or female, and not necessarily sexually. Charmer politicians seduce whole countries.

An adult child of an alcoholic or other dysfunction gravitates to what he knows, to that with which he's experienced in dealing, regardless of the outcome. Survival becomes an appealing excitement.

- A healthy person seeks to *be* good.
- A Charmer seeks to be *perceived* as good because he *desperately needs to believe he is good, because he fears he isn't.*
- A con artist seeks to be *perceived* as good in order to get what he wants.

The farther along the continuum a Charmer moves, the more he is into himself and the less he is capable of empathy for others *and* the deeper the pathology and danger to others and to important decisions.

Bill Clinton was a Charmer up to the point of losing the race for reelection as governor of Arkansas. At that point, he realized the door to his political aspirations would close unless he made a decision to use what had always worked for him to regain his position. He was no longer just doing what came naturally for him, he decided to use those tools deliberately for his end goal. With that decision, he ceased to be a Charmer and became a con artist.

Like Tony in one of our previous profiles, Clinton has his followers who compromise their own integrity to defend him and whose pride stands in the way of their seeing the truth.

WHAT IS THE ANSWER?

FOR THE CHARMER:
PATHOLOGY OR REDEMPTION?

I T IS A DIFFICULT CHOICE even to want recovery. For Charmers who make this choice and who follow through, life will seem mundane, dull, and far less exciting. Why would anyone choose to give up the ability to manipulate people and situations, give up being the center of one's own world, and forfeit the seemingly easy life these things bring, exchanging them for being ordinary and working for success? It takes so much longer to do things that way!

For most Charmers, it will never make sense to do this. Usually, the only reason people choose to change is because their present pain outweighs their fear of change. Part of that fear is of the long, agonizing ordeal it takes to change, including the constant work of self-monitoring and submitting to accountability to others. The pain of discovering the absence of integrity in their behaviors will not be enough for most Charmers to want to change; they are masters of rationalization. But it is their only hope.

The keys to recovery from the Charmer or from being the Charmer are the same as the alcoholic or any addiction process: awareness, insight, and choice. Because the Charmer is in the dark about how he is abusing himself and others, he must have forced intervention, a moment of truth from which he cannot escape.

An intervention is an event that intrudes into the life, grabbing one's attention in a way that cannot be ignored. It may be, but does not have to be, a formal, staged event. Actually, there are many interventions along life's way if one will only see them. Such an event may be a loss of great significance, such as a person or a job, or it may entail exposure. An intervention may come in the form of a threat to someone important in one's life, a religious or philosophical conversion, or any number of significant emotional events.

At that point, a person makes a choice—the most important choice of his life. Ideally, in a healthy growing-up process, there are many interventions along the way, which should catch one's attention. But if a person's maturity and integrity levels are low enough, and if his skills are good enough to avoid or escape the interventions or consequences of bad behavior, such an individual will just keep going. This person's only hope is that someone somewhere along the way will be able *fully* to grab his attention.

If he just "doesn't get it," if he really cannot grasp the truth of the intervention (which would indicate the beginning of pathology, crossing the line of sanity), he will continue as always. From this point, we only can hope that he will never accelerate his behaviors across that line to the criminal level and into pathology to the degree of no longer being in control of himself. The point at which he is no longer able to handle or manage his growing pathology is the point of crossing that line. The psychopath doesn't know and doesn't care about hurting or destroying others.

It is not enough to say you are sorry. For someone with integrity or the desire for it, there will be a sense of remorse for the pain he's caused others, followed by a willingness to make amends and the changes necessary to be responsible and accountable. Being responsible involves making a choice to do the right thing, including to be responsible or not.

If the intervention is understood and given lip service for change but the behaviors continue, then the Charmer has knowingly changed directions. He is no longer a Charmer, but is now a con artist. He knows exactly what he's doing.

Continuium

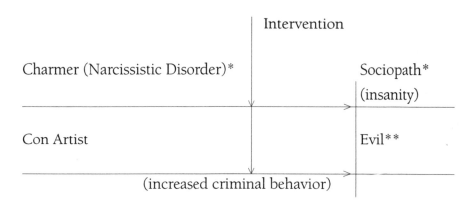

---

* For professional diagnostic characteristics of each disorder, see pages 342-351.[12]

   The Diagnostic and Statistical Manual of Mental Disorders (DSM IV), published by the American Psychiatric Association, cautions that "a Personality Disorder diagnosis should be made only when the characteristic features are typical of the person's long-term functioning and are not limited to discrete episodes of illness." (pg.335).[13] It also states, "many people exhibit traits that are not limited to a single Personality Disorder." (pg. 336) There are certain characteristics that overlap from one disorder to another.[14, 15]

** A good example is Nicolai Carpathia in the *Left Behind* series.

The Charmer *doesn't know* and *doesn't care*. The con artist *knows* but *doesn't care*. There are points of intervention along the way that both the Charmer and the con artist may choose to ignore. If and when the stakes become high enough or the interference with what they want becomes big enough, and the increasing pathology is no longer manageable, each can cross the line from sanity to pathology (insanity), and become a sociopath (Charmer) or give himself over to evil (con artist). At the point of intervention at which the Charmer begins to understand what he's doing, but then chooses to continue his behaviors because they work for him, he has then crossed the line from Charmer to con artist. He is then without any excuse whatsoever for his behavior and cannot plead ignorance. Both may continue on their path and never cross the line of pathology; in fact, most don't.

For both the Charmer and con artist, intervention is the pivotal point. Will it be pathology or redemption? The choice is his and his alone. If he makes the *good* choice, it will change his life, his relationships, and his self-image. (If these steps seem familiar, it's because they are adapted from the Alcoholics Anonymous twelve-step program.)[16]

The first step is recognizing that life is not really as manageable as you have believed; it involves seeing your own hurt and the pain of others realistically.

The second step is admitting you can't change it all by yourself. "His Majesty, The Baby" cannot rear himself. He is in need of reality, a healthy community of caregivers and receivers, and a power greater than himself. False pride has caused him to seek ways to create significance for himself because he fears he has no significance. This step says that a person's significance has already come from God. The seeker's part is merely to accept this as true and to cease his own struggling.

The third step is to make a choice to begin living honestly, dealing with truth and reality and being willing to be held accountable for your behaviors.

The fourth step is to make a searching and fearless inventory of your life for truth, especially your motives.

The fifth step is to admit to yourself and to others what you are doing.

The sixth step is to become willing to be held accountable for your motives and your behaviors.

The seventh step (which includes 7, 8, and 9 of the twelve steps) is to clean up the messes you've made, to make amends, and (where possible) to make restitution to those hurt by your self-centeredness.

The last step (which includes 10, 11, and 12 of the twelve steps) is to continue this process throughout your life and to be an example of the possibility of change, maturity, and integrity.

Addicts have become incapable of learning and changing without help from something or Someone beyond themselves. The addicted person keeps reaching for the same stimuli again and again, trying to make the result of the stimuli change so he won't have to. What contradiction!

Alcoholics Anonymous claims that the rate of recidivism (relapse) for alcoholics, as with most addictions, is almost 95 percent. That's pretty discouraging. However, the 5 percent or more that do recover are worth the efforts made by everyone. The ripple effect of people hurt by alcoholism or any addiction is far wider than just the person addicted. The Charmer and the con artist are also addicts to varying degrees. Their addiction is to their "self" and to whatever it takes to support their habit.

The con artist—since he knows what he's doing, has no conscience about it, and doesn't care who he hurts—must be forcibly stopped.

His activities have always been illegal to some extent, whether petty or serious crimes. Short of a religious or philosophical conversion, he will never change. He must be contained. If the Charmer's behavior crosses legal lines, he, too, must be contained. At the point of breaking the law, you may as well throw away the key; the chances of recovery are that bad.

More often, the Charmer inflicts a different kind of pain. He, too, is hurting, but his attempts to self-medicate are crimes of the heart against others, while merely masking his wounds temporarily.

Neither con artist nor Charmer has true remorse. Remorse + change = repentance. Dr. Laura Schlessinger said it well in her column in the *Detroit Free Press* on May 14, 1998:[17]

The qualities of repentance are:

1. responsibility—recognize the wrong done
2. regret—true remorse for the pain and problems caused
3. resolve—commit never to repeat the act
4. repair the damage, or at least sincerely apologize.

There must be repentance, or there is no redemption, only pathology. Both the Charmer and the con artist are adept at convincing their audiences that they have changed. That's how they ended up where they are. It takes superior scrutiny to make a good judgment as to whether or not their repentance is true. Only strict accountability will prove whether a correct decision was made to trust them again.

With most people, we trust them until they violate that trust. With an uncovered Charmer or con artist, they will forever be proving their right to be trusted. It is part of their recovery. We are fools and enablers if we allow them off the hook merely because of their proclamation of repentance. Lying has been their successful method of operation. The measure of their repentance is *their* willingness to remain accountable.

A person who has integrity will not be insulted by being held accountable. Both the recovering addict and those trying to assist them by holding them accountable know how easily the addict can successfully slip back into lying. The recovering addict will appreciate the commitment of his accountability partners in the long-term goal of recovery.

If virtue is not truly seen as its own reward, the addict has not "gotten it." It is not a question of whether or not God can change someone or the most despicable of behaviors. Of course, He can and does, all the time. It's not about Him. This is about the odds against certain people's willingness to comprehend and respond. Statistics and reality show us that these people have a more difficult time seeing and accepting truth. To fail to recognize this reality is to fail them and to jeopardize ourselves.

Mike Jackson and David Garvin—founders and facilitators of Alternatives to Domestic Aggression, one of the best programs for domestic-violence offenders—state that the percentage of their participants who really "get it" and change their attitude and behavior is less than 5 percent, about the same as the alcoholic.

Jackson and Garvin are good at what they do. They confront, they cannot be conned, and they hold strict accountability. Their pioneer work in their field has earned them a place on the task force of batter intervention services standards of the governor of the state of Michigan; Garvin is cochair of this task force. Both men have been honored with various awards.

As with alcoholics, the importance of even the possibility of change is that no matter how bad the odds, hope is always worth the effort. That is the purpose of this work. It is first of all for those victimized by Charmers, because they hurt the most and deepest, but it is also for the Charmers, too, if they will listen.

The goal is not just to expose and condemn Charmers, but rather to show them where they are, where they are headed, and a better way of getting their needs met. Most will never listen, much less hear or see the reality. They are very comfortable with a method of operation that works in their minds and sustains them in their imaginary significance.

Recovery rate for the Charmer or the con artist is slim. Even so, the pain and misery rate for them and their victims is too high to give up on addressing the problem.

But for this reason, every Charmer or con artist must be assumed to be incapable of change. It's the only protection for others. For that slim percentage who do change, we can grant exceptions to the rules and rejoice while we go on holding them accountable.

FOR THE CHARMED:
VICTIM OR RECOVERY?

A TRUE DEFINITION of *victim* is "one who does not take personal responsibility in a situation." Developing and exercising the ability to respond appropriately—in a healthy, proactive (rather than reactive) way—is how we take responsibility for ourselves.

Being victimized can make you a victim, but remaining a victim is a choice. Will you be bitter and continue being controlled by the victimizer? Will you remain a loyal waif, loving the cad—this narcissistic mixture of foolishness and grandiosity—despite everything? Or will you turn the resulting anger into motivation for changing yourself or the situation?

For the most part, we victims are nice people. Yes, I'm one of those who has been victimized by both a Charmer and a con artist. Most of us will be victimized at one time or another, whether in a relationship, in a marriage, in a business venture, or in getting caught up in a crusade or cult.

We are good, trusting people, sometimes inexperienced. We just look for the best in people and want to believe them until they give reason not to believe them. We are too kind and too forgiving for our own good. We are not simply naive, masochistic individuals. The Charmer is a master at deception, so it may take a very long time for us to see the reality. Only when we have that moment of *Aha!*—that moment of great discovery—will we suddenly have new insight and be able to see everything clearly through new eyes. From that point, truth will continue to unveil itself, layer by layer.

We will then wonder why no one else sees what we see. We will recognize the Charmer's or con artist's thought pattern and rationale and shake our heads. We can't make them see. We feel frustrated that they will never see what we see until they have their own *Aha!* We can only tell them our own experience and trust that it will remain in their memory to validate their own moment of enlightenment, if it ever comes.

Ultimately, we want more for the Charmer, con artist, or codependent than they want for themselves. We see their potential and want to help them achieve it. They want what they want with the fastest shortcut, regardless of the cost. We *want* to lift them up, but they *need* to bring us down in order to feel good about themselves and to feel justified.

The depth of victimization or involvement may vary, depending on many things: age, experience, emotional involvement, perceived credibility of the Charmer or con artist, and our own ego strength. Primarily, we simply are unaware of the motives of people who look normal and charming but who have a hidden agenda. We are the kind of people who are trusting because we are trustworthy. We believe in people and expect the best from them because we give them our best. We don't realize we are out of control of our own lives until the ground on which we stand caves in to a tunnel that's been dug beneath us.

If men, rather than women, are more often Charmers or con artists, then women are more often victims and enablers. While that may allow some sympathy for women, there is also a level of responsibility which they must assume. (In no way is this to be used to blame the victim. Predators—male or female—are still without excuse and should be held accountable.)

As noted earlier, while males are socialized to be aggressive in pursuit of goals, females are socialized to be forgiving and nurturing. There are exceptions to this, exceptions in which roles are reversed. Besides socialization, there are inborn gender differences, which support this. The Charmer has taught his or her victim to feel beyond what is rational or healthy to feel, while the Charmer feels little at all. It is an issue of predator and victim depending on the respective male or female position in the mix.

Neither females nor males are to be faulted for these cherished qualities. The very fiber and stability of society depend on them. However, when people do not allow themselves to learn from facts, and they go on being led, instead, solely by their hearts and emotions, they cooperate in setting themselves up to be people of whom advantage can be taken.

This *does not* include a person's having been seduced, lied to, intimidated, or threatened. It *does* include, for example, the foolishness of women being the strongest supporters of a Bill Clinton and admirers of his long-suffering wife, who continues to "stand by her man," regardless of what she says about herself to the contrary. Who is more deluded: Hillary or the women who support her or who continue to support Bill Clinton?

It's primarily women who bash the foolish, naive, star-struck Monica (who certainly is not blameless) rather than see any imbalance of power in that liaison. What are these female supporters thinking? They aren't. They're only feeling sentimental idealism, devoid of any truth to balance their conclusions. They are compromising principle for perceived legislation on their behalf from a leader who violates his own rhetoric about the protection of women and their freedom from exploitation.

These are the same women who are blind to what their sick kind of loyalty says to Chelsea or to any other child watching such a scenario in their household. For all the strength and independence Hillary has always fought to maintain, she is mush in the hands of a repeated lying, cheating, oops-I-got-caught-but-it-doesn't-matter Charmer.

It leaves a child to wonder:

Is this how men are supposed to behave or be allowed to behave?

Is this what women are supposed to tolerate? Is that what women are for?

Is marriage supposed to be easy for men and hard and demeaning for women?

There is a difference between someone making a foolish mistake and someone making a career of foolish mistakes. The first is about being human. The second is about character failure. A woman who continues to defend an indefensible relationship destroys her own credibility.

The Charmer remains in your life until you unveil him, and even then he will stay as long as you let him. His goal is your admiration of him, as well as his own release from being held accountable for anything. When you finally come to your senses, *you do not owe a Charmer anything—not pity, not another chance, not the benefit of any doubt!* You would not give any of those things to a snake or a rodent in your path.

But don't be fooled that you can't fall into the same trap again. That charm is still what we are drawn to, whether it makes sense or not. We, too, need a method of accountability. We need to forgive ourselves most of all and not punish ourselves.

With a con artist, the deception is more difficult to detect. By the time their deeds have been discovered, they are no longer around. If they weren't really good at what they do, they couldn't be con artists. Even very clever, perceptive people can be conned. A certain amount of engineering of circumstances has been set into place to support the con operation. His plan is well thought-out and executed and is only discovered when a crime is unraveled. By then, he has taken his booty and left.

Whether you are recovering from a Charmer or a con artist, remember that he has fouled and desecrated your nest. He has, in essence, defecated in your food dish, while he remains intact, looking good. Don't be surprised when others blame you for being a victim. It won't make sense, but that's their way of reassuring themselves it could never happen to them (all the while, fearing it could). Don't be alarmed if you find yourself believing that fallacy. After all, you've been carefully trained to doubt your own perspective.

Just as pain is most often the starting point for the Charmer's or con artist's recovery, so the pain we feel as victims must finally outweigh the addictive roller-coaster ride of exhilarating highs and debilitating lows, before we are able to make the decision to extract ourselves from the Charmer or con artist and finally own our own lives. We've been addicted to them. This life-on-the-edge excitement we feel in being with them is similar to the gambling addiction and is equally hard to break.

It's embarrassing to realize and admit you've been taken in, charmed, or conned. Part of the humiliation is in realizing you've participated in your own victimization. There will even be people who will say, "It's your own fault. How could you not see through him [or her]?" Even if they don't say it, that's what we hear.

The bigger the audience of a Charmer (e.g., O. J. Simpson) or con artist (e.g., Bill Clinton), the longer it takes to catch on to them and the more resistant people are to acknowledge what they see or to demand accountability. The collective ego is at stake. However, if we will allow them to do so, these high-profile Charmers and con artists can serve to awaken our sleeping perceptions regarding our own lives.

For victims, all this is not a matter of blame. We are not to blame for being used, taken advantage of, or victimized. However, we have been wounded by it, and we alone are responsible for our own healing and for firmly setting up accountability for the predator.

There is a period of grieving over the loss of a dream, the sudden drench of ice-cold reality, the anger at the Charmer, the anger at ourselves. We may argue with them and with ourselves, try to bargain, rationalize, or justify, all to lessen the impact. We may become depressed. Grieving all the many losses involved with a Charmer, as well as dealing with the feelings attached to them, complicate the process of reaching a level of acceptance and of being able to heal and go forward. Acceptance is an act of the will and denotes a willingness to go in a different, healthier direction. (This treatise on grief is expanded in my book *Starting Again*.)[18]

After the merry-go-round relationship, the recovery process is the same as from any other addiction. We, the charmed, have been addicted to the Charmer. He was addicted to himself. Together we resemble a dog chasing its tail.

Charmers are envied. They seem to get away with all sorts of things. It seems they could fall into a bucket of horse manure and come out smelling like a rose. Envy alternates with resentment of and anger at Charmers.

"He's the one with the problem. I'm the victim. Why should I have to recover?" That's the exact thinking of children of alcoholics and of those attending Al-Anon (for recovering family and friends of alcoholics). It's the same program. Our lives have become unmanageable, and we now share the problem too. It isn't fair. But that's the way it is.

Victims are subtly trained to *not know* what normal is. They think they are in control. That belief has been encouraged by their perpetrator. Bargains and tradeoffs are nonverbally made. And even though the victim never agreed to them, they are expected to go along, and they find themselves doing so.

When challenged, the Charmer knows how to "mess with your mind" and normalize his actions. He can twist, distort, and tarnish your self-image or your reputation. If the situation gets to a stage of involving the law or the courts, he is able to use and play the courts like strings on a harp. Breaking free is not easy. Even after you have decided to, actually pulling it off is an even greater challenge. Our self-confidence is shattered. Others' confidence in our judgment is eroded. We are immobilized by disbelief and depression. This is a point at which anger can be used positively to motivate change.

If your Charmer has become abusive, genuine fear about the repercussions of leaving is a powerful force. It is even more powerful if you have children. A Charmer knows your spots of vulnerability. It is not uncommon for him to abuse his own children to punish you for leaving him. We see it every day.

With the grieving and healing process, the task is then to learn from our innocence, our naiveté, and even our mistakes. Experience has been an effective teacher.

What should you do if you recognize your involvement with a Charmer or con artist? Run for your life! Whether your experience is quicksand, B'rer Rabbit stuck on Tarbaby, or the frog cooking slowly to death, you *will* be hurt or even destroyed.

If it's a loss of money you're concerned about, that can be replaced; it's just a matter of time. If it's the loss of self, it could take years, if at all. That time is lost forever and it's not replaceable. If there is anything good to be gleaned from this experience, it is your new ability to detect and to become immune to the Charmer. Addicts are never cured—they are only survivors living in recovery.

If your Charmer is a family member from whom you cannot easily separate yourself (or you choose not to), there are three options:

1. Practice consistent tough love. Maintain your autonomy, learning the techniques of assertiveness and detachment from their life choices. Reclaim your own "self."
2. Remove them, if possible, or yourself to a safe distance and love them from there.
3. Learn what healthy boundaries are and maintain them at all cost.

Whichever choice you make will be difficult and sometimes impossible to maintain and may call for acceleration of your uninvolvement or discontinued involvement altogether. The Charmer or con artist in your life won't accept that loss of control. Either they will leave for greener pastures, or they may have to be forcibly removed if they become abusive. *They won't change! You* must change *your* response to them.

The cost of your survival—financial, emotional, or physical—will be the loss, partially or totally, of the Charmer from your life. We don't really want that, though. We really want them to magically change. That's why we live in our denial, hoping against hope. It's a very tough choice.

Now we need to know the new direction toward which we must head.

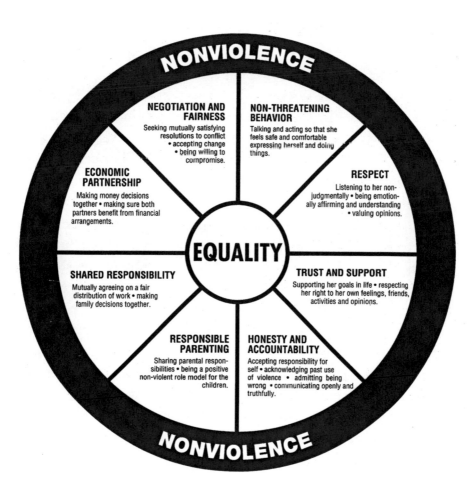

DOMESTIC ABUSE INTERVENTION PROJECT
202 East Superior Streat
Duluth, Minnesota 55802
218-722-2781

What About the Children?

This book has been about adult-to-adult relationships. What about the children of Charmers? What do they learn?

The role models children have are their most important lessons in life, the most important of whom are their primary caregivers: their parents. What people teach a child is very important, but how they live speaks louder than what they say. Little children automatically see their parents as all-knowing and trustworthy. Even those who have been abused want to stay with their parents. They live with the hope that the parent will be loving to them next time.

With normal, healthy development through childhood to becoming an adult, children learn the human frailties of adults, including their parents'. If there has been consistency and a balance between love and discipline (*discipline* means "to teach," not "to punish," and teaching includes natural consequences of choices), then children will have developed the personal ego strength to become their own person, to separate out their love for their parents from the mistakes their parents have made and from their deficiencies. Children will begin to chart their own course, having learned from both the positives and the negatives of their caregivers.

It is easy to see the difficulty a child could have growing up with a Charmer. There are many mixed messages through which the child must sort. Children are imitators, especially if what they imitate works. Their young minds see only the immediate results, not the unseen or future consequences.

Children are also imitators as a way of showing their love for their parents or for others they admire. Just watch how children play. Whether it's with Barbie dolls, cowboys, or space invaders, they are mimicking. The tennis shoes they must have, the clothing fads they follow, or the hairstyle that is just like their idol's—these all speak to their homage.

Emulating the same-sex parent is also a means of role identification and of validation of their own blossoming femininity or masculinity. It is very hard for a child to be objective about that parent. It's like critiquing himself or herself. They desperately want and need validation of themselves, and in their formative years, that parent is their validation. If the parent is a Charmer or a victim, think of the messages the children get!

Public figures are important role models, whether or not they think they are or want to be. As children move away from their parents in developing their own autonomy, they begin watching more closely other adults and peers to find the direction in which to take their own lives.

The stronger their family and the healthier their parental guidance, the more likely they will choose other good adults to follow. It is not impossible for a child to go astray from a good upbringing, and it is not impossible for a child to find his own good way from a bad or inadequate upbringing.

Children of Charmers and their victims are victims, too, and they need a program and a place to work through the false information about life they've received, just as children of alcoholics do. They have to have a recovery time and process, as do Charmers and adult victims. Many will simply follow what they know. Others will determine to be all the things they never had in a healthy parent.

For the children's sake, we owe it to them and to our society to live healthy, balanced, appropriate lives. It saves everyone having to spend a lot more energy later to fix the resulting problems—if it is even possible to fix them. The children are watching us.

A Self-Test:
Charmed or Charmer?

S ocrates said that the unexamined life is not worth living. Whether that examination is of ourselves or of someone else, it's a good guideline for a relationship. A wise man seeks to be critiqued, to monitor his motives and behaviors. This is the key to integrity and character. It is also the key to good mental health. It is a combination of self-monitoring and seeing our own reflection from the eyes of others.

• A true friend cares more about your character than your comfort. Confrontation is to strengthen and to soften.[19]

• "Faithful are the wounds of a friend, but the kisses of an enemy are deceitful" (Prov. 27:6).

• Character is what we are when no one is watching and we would not get caught. It's not just what a man does occasionally, or in the limelight, but what he is in the main. To be human is to make mistakes. However, it is by the consistency of one's life that one is defined.

Oswald Chambers said that a crisis does not make character; but reveals character.[20]

What one does with his mistakes is very telling of his character. Hiding, rationalizing, and justifying are the reactions of the Charmer or con artist. Facing up to responsibilities is a mark of character.

Envy the Charmer? What does he really have? What is the true quality of his life? The one who dies with the most toys wins? The biggest reputation? The most highly acclaimed?

If the negatives are dangerous enough, positives cannot offset them, no matter how beneficial the positives are.[21]

Life is dynamic, not stagnant. It is short. The only lasting thing of value that we leave here on earth or take with us when we die, is our relationships. To make that happen, we have to be willing to give up what we cannot keep to gain what we can never lose. [22]

Life is about growing, moving forward. Those are internal things. There is a genuine peace that comes with the contentment of living life well, with virtue and integrity. The Charmer's peace is his delusion. The Charmer is not growing. His life is surface, external, a process of deterioration. Just to maintain the facade, he must sink ever deeper and deeper into his sickness. Life will never change for him unless he changes who he fundamentally is.

It takes years of recovery to really grasp that and to believe it—to believe it enough to stake your life on it. It's difficult to walk away from artificial highs and pick up the mantle of work and healthy living. It takes the things learned in recovery to see that Charmers only *appear* to win.

Susan (in Tony's story) saw that. Her anger and resentment gave way to seeing that she had the final justice. Her life grew, blossomed, and became expansive by comparison to what it had been and to what Tony's still is. Tony was never able to grasp the concept of character or integrity. He is still there, locked in a revolving door that just goes round and round. He knew no real remorse, so nothing could change. The same is true with the other case studies.

The hallmark of good mental health is the well-balanced life. Like four legs on a table, our lives are divided into four main parts:

1. *work*—what we do to feel a sense of accomplishment and satisfaction and pride in ourselves
2. *family and friends*— those who support us and with whom we have a sense of relationship
3. *values*—the statement of our personhood, who we really are inside (may or may not include religion)
4. *recreation*—what we do to renew, refresh, and re-create ourselves for the sake of the other three parts.

If one of those legs is shorter than the others, the whole table of our lives will wobble, be unstable. If the table is bumped, anything on top will fall off unless it is moved as far as possible away from the short leg. Two or three short legs increases the possibility of things falling off.

If one of the legs is longer than the rest, nothing placed anywhere on the table will stay there. Having one leg longer than the other three often indicates an addiction. Nothing is in balance. The table can no longer function for the purpose it was intended.

That same sense of balance is important in discerning, or being wise, in identifying a healthy person for a relationship. Through our study of the Charmer, his flip side (the abuser), and the con artist, one thing becomes obvious: they are all out of balance. Besides the distortions in thinking and behaving, their concept of love and truth are out of sync. Love is a river that requires knowledge and discernment as its boundaries.

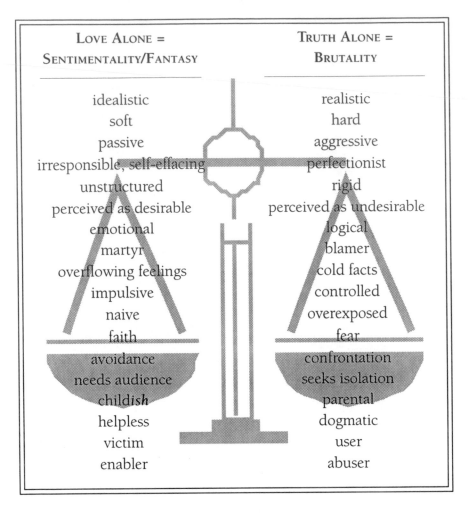

LOVE ALONE = SENTIMENTALITY/FANTASY	TRUTH ALONE = BRUTALITY
idealistic	realistic
soft	hard
passive	aggressive
irresponsible, self-effacing	perfectionist
unstructured	rigid
perceived as desirable	perceived as undesirable
emotional	logical
martyr	blamer
overflowing feelings	cold facts
impulsive	controlled
naive	overexposed
faith	fear
avoidance	confrontation
needs audience	seeks isolation
childish	parental
helpless	dogmatic
victim	user
enabler	abuser

Love without truth is sentimentality (fantasy). Truth without love is brutality. (See chart above.) The balance between love and truth equals the following:

- maturity
- integrity
- reality
- responsibility
- wholeness

206

- completeness
- health
- objectivity
- accountability
- genuineness
- child*like*ness
- teachability
- spirituality

It would be unconscionable to present a problem without offering hope for solution. These are not easy concepts to grasp. They can be discouraging unless countered with options for relief and hope.

Human nature causes us to look for quick paths to happiness. As stated before, happiness is about externals, happenings. It is a surface experience and is short lived. Joy is internal, intrinsic, and eternal. Author Tim Hansel says that joy is peace dancing and peace is joy at rest.

Where the Charmer and con artist are concerned, love alone, with its fantasy, sentimentality and wishful thinking, is their tool to control their world to quickly make life pleasant and comfortable for themselves. They would rather live in a comfortable lie than balance love with convicting truth. They only want happiness. Victims have been programmed to believe their happiness will come through a person who appears to know the way. Both are lost as long as they continue in the same downward spiral.

What the human heart longs for is joy, peace, and contentment at a deep, lasting level. That only comes through both love and truth balanced in a life.

Recovery is based on the interjection of truth to:

- awaken us to the need for truth

- provide the tools for applying truth to the unhealthy parts of our lives, and
- free us to live life at a deeper level that satisfies our soul's search for peace.

The mixture of love and truth set in motion a process of discovery, change, and healing. It is the only healthy and fulfilling answer. There are no shortcuts to joy.

ENDNOTES

1. American Psychiatric Association: Diagnostic and Statistical Manual of Mental Disorders, Fourth Edition, Revised. Washington, DC, American Psychiatric Association, 1994.

2. DSM IV, p. 358.

3. DSM IV, p. 359.

4. Dr. Susan Forward and Joan Torres, Men Who Hate Women and the Women Who Love Them, New York: Bantam Books, 1986.

5. Susan Faludi, "The Betrayal of the American Man", Newsweek Magazine,. pp. 48-59, from her book Stiffed: The Betrayal of the American Man, (New York: William Morrow & Co., Inc.)

6. Steven Naifeh and Gregory White Smith, <u>Why Can't Men Open Up?</u> (New York: C.N. Potter, Crow Publishers, 1984).

7. Mel Small, "JFK's Wild Ride", <u>The Detroit Free Press</u>, October 10, 1993: a review of <u>President Kennedy: Profile of Power</u>, by Richard Reeves, (New York: Simon & Schuster, 1993).

8. Dr. William E. Hapworth, Dr. Mada Hapworth, and Joan Rattner Heilman, "Mom Loved You Best", 1993. Reprint arrangement with Viking Penguin, a division of Penguin Books USA, Inc. and reprinted in an article on office siblings in <u>Redbook Magazine</u>, September, 1993.

9. Dr. Laura Schlessinger, <u>The Detroit Free Press</u>, June 11, 1998.

10. Dr. M. Scott Peck, <u>People of the Lie</u>, (New York: Simon & Schuster, 1992), p. 197.

11. "Obstruction and Abuse: A Pattern", <u>The Wall Street Journal</u>, February 12, 1998.

12. DSM IV, pp. 329-334.

13. DSM IV, p. 330.

14. DSM IV, p. 335.

15. Tim LaHaye and Jerry B. Jenkins, <u>Left Behind</u> series, (Wheaton, Illinois: Tyndale House Publishers, Inc., 1995).

16. "The Twelve Step Program", <u>Alcoholics Anonymous</u>.

17. Dr. Laura Schlessinger, <u>The Detroit Free Press</u>, May 14, 1998.

18. Sandra Scott, <u>Starting Again: A Divorce Recovery Program</u>, (Nashville: Discipleship Resources, The United Methodist Church, 1997, pp. 11-59.)

19. Dr. David Augsburger, <u>Caring Enough to Confront</u>, (Ventura, California: Regal Books, 1985.)

20. Oswald Chambers, <u>My Utmost for His Highest</u>, (Westwood, N.J.: Barbour and Company, Inc., 1963.)

21. Dr. Richard A. Swenson, <u>Margin</u>, (Colorado Springs, Colorado: Navpress, 1992.)

22. Elizabeth Elliott, <u>Through the Gates of Splendor</u>, (Wheaton, Illinois: Tyndale House Publishers, 1986), paraphrase of words of her husband, slain missionary, Jim Elliott.

OTHER REFERENCES

A & E Biographies, videos – O.J. Simpson
                         Leona Helmsley
                         Eva Peron
                         Bill Clinton

Baker, Beth, "Profile: Michael Gurian, Helping Boys Become Men". AARP Bulletin, March 2000

Beattie, Melody, Beyond Codependency (San Francisco: Harper & Row Publishers, 1989).

Beattie, Melody, Codependent No More (New York: Harper & Row Publishers, 1987).

Dalby, Gordon, Healing the Masculine Soul, (Dallas: Word Publishing, 1988).

Hansel, Tim, You Gotta Keep Dancin', (Elgin, Illinois: David C. Cook Publishing, 1985),

Kiley, Dr. Dan, The Peter Pan Syndrome (New York: Avon Books, 1983).

Lowen, Dr. Alexander, <u>Narcissism: Denial of the True Self</u> (New York: Collier Books, 1985).

McCullough, Colleen, <u>The Thornbirds</u> (New York: Harper & Row, 1977). (Excerpts from the movie)

Mitchell, Margaret, <u>Gone With the Wind</u>, (New York: Warner Books, 1994). (Excerpts from the movie)

Runyon, Damon, <u>Guys and Dolls</u>, (Philadelphia: J.B. Lippincott Company, 1931-35).

Smalley, Gary and Trent, Dr. John, <u>The Two Sides of Love</u>, (Pamona, California: Focus on the Family, 1990).

Stowell, Dr. Joseph M., <u>Perilous Pursuits: Our Obsession With Significance</u> (Chicago: Moody Press, 1994).

Sandra Scott, a Licensed Professional Counselor, has been in private practice for fifteen years, specializing in individual and family relationship issues. She is a conference speaker and a certified divorce mediator. Another of her titles *Starting Again: A Divorce Recovery Program* is currently in use by the United Methodist Church.

Having developed an expertise in pre-divorce and pre-marital counseling, Sandra has conducted numerous seminars on abuse, which are primarily directed at educating church leaders and congregations in recognizing and responding appropriately to all aspects of this major problem. Sandra also has been actively involved in singles ministry leadership for fifteen years.

Pleasant
Word

To order additional copies of this title:
Please visit our web site at
www.pleasantwordbooks.com

If you enjoyed this quality custom published book,
drop by our web site for more books and information.

www.winepressgroup.com

"Your partner in custom publishing."

Printed in the United States
212351BV00001B/205/A